Mother Church

What the Experience of Women Is Teaching Her

SALLY CUNNEEN

Paulist Press   New York/Mahwah, N.J.

The excerpt from "Six Night Letters" by Thomas Merton is taken from *The Collected Poems of Thomas Merton,* copyright © 1968 by the Abbey of Gethsemane, Inc. and reprinted by permission of New Directions Publishing Corp.

Cover art: *Madonna del Parto* by Piero della Francesca, Arezzo, Italy.

Library of Congress Cataloging in Publication Data

Cunneen, Sally.
    Mother church: what the experience of women is teaching her/ Sally Cunneen.
      p. cm.
    Includes bibliographical references.
    ISBN 0-8091-3265-6 (pbk.)
    1. Church. 2. Motherhood—Religious aspects—Catholic Church. 3. Catholic Church—Doctrines. I. Title.
BX1746.C866 1991   91-23664
                                                          CIP

Published by Paulist Press
997 Macarthur Blvd.
Mahwah, New Jersey 07430

Printed and Bound in the United States of America.

Contents

1

A New Focus on People-Making

This is a book about our need to grow up humanly, the necessity to pay attention to *this* world as central to our religious obligation today. Because contemporary technology is so much more developed than our ability to understand ourselves or to work together, the very survival of the planet now depends on more conscious, creative attention to human development and relationships.

Since I am a Roman Catholic, it is also in some degree a book about the church. I hope, however, to be addressing a broader audience than my co-religionists, if only as a partial repayment to the many Protestant, Jewish, and humanist neighbors and thinkers who have contributed so much to the perspective I hope to communicate. So when I refer to "church," I hope it's understood as one whose doors are open; even if I am drawing on such a traditionally Catholic image as "mother church," I hope to reimagine it, enriched by its ancient meaning newly illuminated by contemporary discoveries and challenges.

And it is also a book about mothering. This is partly because I believe that the church—and many of our other institutions—have much to learn from a more realistic understanding of the experience of mothers, available from

1

their point of view for the first time. But my deepening familiarity with the difficulties mothers have in being good mothers gradually led me to think of mothering as a function, something quite different from a role or indeed from physical motherhood. Of course, it is easy for me to understand why many women today, in a reaction against the way in which both church and society tried to limit their options, may at first believe I am not talking to them: some don't want to be mothers, and those who do correctly refuse to allow motherhood to define their total existence, especially when it has been seen as a vocation for all women and misunderstood for so long by cultural and ecclesial authorities. But mothering, in contrast, is important for all of us, whether men or women; it is something we have to do throughout our lives, for ourselves and for each other. In their different ways modern developmental psychologists and the greatest saints and doctors of the church insist on our need to grow throughout the various stages of our lives; if we are to become authentic people, we have to integrate what we believe with all that we know and are.

Just as many women have horror stories to tell about how they (or their mothers, or aunts, or friends) experienced motherhood as a trap, many (not just women) have horror stories to tell about the church. Unfortunately, although there are exaggerations and a few have succumbed to bitterness, in neither case have the stories just been made up. I have no intention of dwelling on them in this book, but I am well aware that too many Catholics—including long-time churchgoers and graduates of Catholic schools—will be quick to say that the church they experienced was not asking them to grow, was not leading them to greater freedom, was not teaching them how to take responsibility for building the more just and peaceful society it advocated. They may have heard that the Second Vatican Council defined the church as "the people of God," but in terms of the reality they encountered in their parish or their school this seemed like another empty slogan. Too little, too late. There may be a wealth of contemporary biblical scholarship that shows we are meant to be co-creators of our church and our world, but not enough has been done to give such teaching flesh and blood. That is why the religious identity of many Catholics seems to stop at a childhood stage, followed by adolescent rebellion or passive submission, not connected to their overall development as social, cultural people; at best, we find our way to a private spirituality that does not relate us to the wider community. Too much of what is said and done in the name of the church doesn't help us think and act positively or creatively, faithful to our tradition but learning from those who have different beliefs and behavior patterns.

When I employ the image of mother church, therefore, even many Catholics react negatively; they think of a nagging mother who accented the negative—"Keep away from sin"—and passed on her fears of what was outside her own fortress of authority. Such a mother was apt to be so intent on inculcating doctrinal truths and mandating goodness that she made a real relationship with her grown-up children impossible. However unintentionally, she also communicated a most un-Christian fear of sex. The overall result was an experience of religion that controlled and limited people's natural spiritual experiences; in the process many almost lost the vital connections between themselves, the earth, and each other that give ritual and worship their meaning.

What they—and the rest of us—need, I have come to believe, is a mother who listens to them, shares herself with them, and, in the process, enables them. Long after we've lost our physical mothers, all of us still need to give and receive that kind of mothering, helping each other rediscover those vital connections, integrating our spirituality with our actual lives, personalities and experiences. Only then can we come to know better who we are and what we might do as "the people of God" in a time when understanding and choice rather than automatic assent is essential if faith is to remain alive.

I know this need for connections because of my own painful struggle to grow as a human being and a Christian while trying to bring up four children. I saw that my children needed to trust the world and themselves in order to be able to make human decisions that were also moral and spiritual, in order to be both free and loving. It took me all too long to break through the pat definitions I'd received in childhood, which seemed to divide the universe into good and bad, secular and sacred. With millions of others I passed through a time when the apparently stable notions of family and mother were eroding, while leaders in both church and society went on offering ideals of womanhood that seemed increasingly irrelevant. Recent research has shown, for example, that the silent woman, long idealized in the church, is often a person unable to make the moral decisions faith calls for.

Perhaps the best justification for my emphasis on the experience of mothers is that mothers cannot help but know that they make lots of mistakes; indeed, they often need a good deal of support to assure them that they haven't completely failed. Mothers, of course, can be vain and superficial, but they would never claim infallibility. All I hope to do in this book is to start an honest conversation between groups who do not usually have a chance to share information with one another useful to themselves, the church and the wider community. If at first it seems strange that I draw on the image of the church as mother, I can only say that I have found it useful in integrating my own thinking and behavior. Since reconciliation of spirituality within human resources and concern for integrated human development is also our common need, it seems a fruitful way to carry on this conversation.

The idea of sharing my own reeducation in this book first came to me more than ten years ago when I began to give courses in contemporary mothering, at the community college where I teach, in collaboration with two other faculty mothers, an anthropologist and a psychologist. Having learned from our mistakes, we designed our course to tune students in to their own needs as well as their children's. Reviewing the history of parenting and its many contemporary styles, we tried first to evoke our students' experiences, asked them to do a written reevaluation of their experience in the light of assigned readings and group discussion, and tried to help them make future choices in keeping with their real strengths and beliefs. ·

The course, which was given in one of the rooms the college rented above a local 5 & 10, included a good deal of role-playing of family arguments, which seemed to make it easier for students to talk honestly with other family members. Dealing with possible conflicts in this way helps people unlearn overly defensive reactions so that they can begin to talk their way to more nurturing relationships. As I listened, memories of repeated and unresolved arguments in my own family flooded my mind. Most of us were seeing patterns of behavior played out in that room that we ourselves had engaged in at one time or another. We could recognize our own tendency to bully, placate or distract as we observed tactics that were clearly preventing this mock family from dealing with their real problems, preventing its members from growing up and growing close.

I'm not sure what particular incident finally convinced me that the ideas that lay behind this class process —in which I was both facilitator and learner—needed to be shared. Perhaps it was the time when a mother reported to us that her teenage children had actually listened to her for the first time in months, though she had previously nagged and nagged. She had convinced herself at last that she should no longer accept total responsibility for the housework and cleaning. She convened a family conference and told everyone how much she wanted to go to college; they would have to work out a common plan for dealing with household chores. It was almost the first time she heard her children and her husband talking to *her,* not as wife or mom, but as a person with a life of her own. She had been afraid of resistance, but she managed to tell her family what she wanted, and they had responded with immediate offers of cooperation. She was grateful to them, of course, but as class discussion continued she also began to realize that what she had done was the best thing possible for them as well.

Fortunately, we always had two or three men in the course. I was particularly impressed by Jim, a father in his mid-thirties who admitted how ashamed he felt at first when he had to stay home with the kids because of a disability, while his wife worked as a nurse. But now he was deeply involved with his daughter's education; he found it more demanding and more fascinating than the work he used to do, and much more important. He began to delight in her lively mind, and he felt his own horizons broaden as he took her to museums and encouraged her to write and paint. As he surrendered his earlier stereotypes of male-female differences, Jim said he was beginning to feel more fully human.

I also remember the day when Helen, stiff with resentment at the husband who had abandoned her with their three children, finally had enough confidence in us to talk frankly about her experiences. Later, as she became more relaxed with her classmates, she told us she felt more confident—and competent—in dealing with her children. She had felt unlovable for so long that at the beginning of the course she could not accept the disinterested concern other students showed for her. She snapped back at the least hint of help or advice, feeling it was either criticism or condescension. The thaw began when she finally realized that these simple gestures of care were non-judgmental.

In each of these instances, I could see an active force at work that differed from our dominant cultural emphasis on competition and success. It surfaced spontaneously in most of the group as they observed and reached out to one another. It seemed to help foster connections between their inner sense of self and their ability to relate to the outer world of reality with a greater sense of direction. I began to use the term "mothering" for what was taking place in that course because these are the very things psychologists tell us good mothers are supposed to do for children. As described in the syllabus, what was going on was solid traditional education, with emphasis on close reading, clear writing, and elementary logic, but an extra dynamic had emerged that was equally important. I knew from my own and my children's experience that enabling people to take charge of their own lives was not a priority in most educational settings, which generally reflected an almost total split between intellect and emotion.

The mothering going on in those courses was a human, not a female activity. Perhaps it should be seen as a human virtue, a self-confidence that facilitates an enlargement of sympathy and leads to thinking and action in the interest of others. Clearly it applies to adult relationships as much as to those between parents and children. Physical mothers are often blamed for not providing it, as if they alone have that responsibility, as if they don't need mothering themselves—as we all do. I am more and more convinced that the concern to provide it is as "natural" to men as to women, even though it is little rewarded in a society still dominated by a masculine authority. In any case, the human suffering caused by the relative neglect of mothering in our culture emerged as a central theme in class discussions.

It was my students that provided the questions that prompted this book. Single mothers who knew they were beyond their depth, young men who were sufficiently sure of themselves to question the macho ideal their neighborhood had taught them, grandmothers who were as willing to confront their bitter memories as to show us photos of their grandchildren, asked the same questions: How can we live together and still be true to ourselves? How can we foster the individuality and well-being of both parents and children? How do we build a community that reaches out to the millions today who are not living in families? These are what I call mothering questions.

Then one day, inevitably, because the church was always central to my concerns, I had to connect these questions with another: Why couldn't the church, which has traditionally called itself a mother, be an effective mediator in helping to answer them? In the securely "secular" environment of a public college we were learning that arbitrary rules, exclusively top-down communication and unshared power were destructive to families. Because the course elicited such deep response, discussion often contained a sub-current bordering on the "ultimate questions" for which the great world religions have long offered responses. It was discouraging to note how few of the students, who came from a variety of religious backgrounds, had significant contact with the spiritual riches of their different traditions. Those who considered themselves Catholics—usually about half the class—were neither bitter nor defiant, but often thought of the church either in terms of private devotion or in terms of a top-down authority, offering unchanging rules to which they were expected to submit out of loyalty, if not fear. Surely there was a sad paradox here: in class our focus was on what our textbook called "people-making," but there was little evidence that the church which had so recently defined itself as "the people of God" had done much to promote the individual development and maturity of those who wished to be its loyal members. Why couldn't this church be a more effective mother?

At first I daydreamed about exercises in straight communication in the parish, with the pastor asking the people what they actually thought of his sermons—better yet, asking them to participate in helping him develop them, perhaps occasionally even giving them. I imagined groups of parishioners meeting with the priests and parish ministers in cross-cultural sensitivity sessions or taking Myers-Briggs tests to improve their ability to work together. I fantasized that Sr. Teresa Kane was having a heart-to-heart talk with the pope and that the Vatican was issuing guidelines for parallel discussions between women and church officials in every diocese. I even dreamed that internationally representative groups of grandparents were replacing curia cardinals and staff at the Vatican, sharing their stories, confessing their disappointments, passing on their hopes for the future.

But then I stopped myself. I was already getting into grandiose schemes, preaching in reverse—as mothers are sometimes known to do. No, something more modest was in order. What had helped me change was the certainty that I *needed* to change. After all, when I started to teach mothering classes, I was quite aware that I had made mistakes as a mother—out of ignorance, a combination of good intentions and lack of self-understanding, because I wasn't sufficiently ready for the challenges of the different world my children faced. Those courses in contemporary mothering gradually taught me what I'd already more than suspected, that I might have done things much better for my children and myself. But I also learned that people *can* change, that it is never too late—that I could still go on to heal some wounds, mine and others, that life extends beyond the family. Perhaps the church, too, could become a wiser mother, echoing Jesus' question: "Who are my mother and my brothers?"

Psychologists tell us that there are both nurturing and troubled families. The church, of course, wants to nurture, but inevitably, like any real family, it provides disabling as well as healing experiences. Although Catholics believe Christ is present in the church, only an infantile faith insists on an angelic institution or a purely spiritual community. We can take heart from the reassurance of therapists who tell us that families can change from troubled to nurturing when its members begin to take responsibility for their lives and share their thinking honestly with one another. Two contrasting attitudes to mothering correlate with the troubled and the nurturing family: the first overprotects and stifles independent growth, the second empowers those it cares for to become independent. Most of us have received and dispensed a good deal of both. Like human mothers, church leaders—who, despite their crucial role and legitimate authority, should never be simply identified with the church—have often given in to the temptation to smother rather than to enable. This is hardly surprising; mothers especially realize how hard it is to recognize that the child is in a new stage of development and is ready for greater independence; they would be the last to forget how thin a line it can be between over-control and an irresponsible absence of supervision. This book is not looking for villains. The truth is that all of us, including mothers, have been raised imperfectly and unconsciously pass on our weaknesses; what is important is that we try to live our lives more consciously. We shouldn't use the authoritarian personality of an individual pastor as a cop-out, or waste our energy lamenting a given Vatican decree. Whether we are young, in mid-life, or already retired, now is the time to integrate our faith with what we know, into the person we are, the life we lead.

We all need mothering in order to give it, but often we must begin by mothering ourselves. That is one of the principal lessons I have learned from contemporary mothers, and it applies to both parents and children, bishops and ordinary churchgoers. Perhaps the best way to begin learning how to mother well is by listening in on the struggles and mistakes of mothers themselves. That is why I air the voices of actual, physical mothers early in this book. Today, perhaps for the first time in history, they are defining themselves and their own task; they are no longer willing to accept the passive, suffering role-ideal so long imposed on them by others. Their struggles, their cries of outrage—even if sometimes expressed in extreme terms —are an important resource which can help us all to see what is needed to make mature, moral decisions, to become authentic selves.

The responsibilities of real mothers also remind us of the responsibility anyone in authority has over others. They give birth to small beings who are totally dependent but filled with incredible potential; it is up to parents—in practice, it has usually been left to mothers—to help them grow in health and wonder, mind, body and spirit together. Sometimes reluctantly, mothers learn to recognize that it is not by avoiding encounters with life but precisely through facing up to them and dealing with them that their children can become responsible, loving grown-ups, able to enjoy life and themselves intelligently because they have developed inner discipline.

In contrast, the church has all too often short-circuited this process of growing up. In its desire to protect its members from error and evil influences, it has sometimes come close to creating an unreal world with unreal boundaries, splitting off emotion from reason rather than fostering a full human response to life. Yet belief in the Incarnation points to the need for just such total response. In our era we have had the visionary example of John XXIII to remind us that the primary work of religion in the modern world is to empower all men and women, including the poorest and least powerful, in decisions that might result in a peaceful, equitable sharing of the earth's resources. He reminded us of the mothering we need to restore to our actions and thinking. Some have followed his example—particularly in the base communities of Latin America—but most of us haven't learned how to deal positively with the world and with each other, even though we say we believe in peace and justice.

Why is it so hard? Well, for one thing because we often give our allegiance to one group, country, race, ideology or religion without recognizing our rootedness in the physical world and our deepest human identity. For another, because the virtues that have accompanied concern for human growth have been arbitrarily relegated to women—considered primarily as potential mothers—by those very forces that have made the decisions leading to our current predicament. Care and concern, like child-raising, have so long been relegated to women that only now are we beginning to question entrenched assumptions as to what is really male and female.

Life experience and teaching others have helped me gain insight into the processes of good mothering in families as well as in church tradition and teaching. Each casts light on the other. Just as "Invisibles" show up magically on the computer when you push the right button, so I came to see cultural and ecclesiastical invisibles I had not noticed before. Revisiting artistic symbols in different periods of history, I saw good mothering as a perennial human need. At the same time, I saw that mothers in recent history were idealized in theory and ignored in reality. Most people in authority have seriously misguided notions of what it takes to raise children well. If mothers are expected to do it, they will need a different education and much more public support. They shouldn't be asked to do it alone, but even if they accept that unfair division of labor, their efforts will have only minor impact in a culture that doesn't value the nurturing, enabling, and sharing needed for effective mothering.

To be successful, real parents have to nurture and protect children, then let them go. They still must share themselves and their resources with their children as adult friends and equals across the generations. To be successful at letting go, however, one must reverse intense, long-cultivated habits and ideas. It is even harder for mothers than fathers. In the Genesis story the Father has already launched us, yet we still need to grow into our responsibilities on this earth.

Could that be why the church has always called herself a mother? If she is, she too may be capable of learning and changing. You have noticed how I call her "she." A shadowy figure of an old, old woman began to take root in my imagination years ago. Gradually she became more and more real, and finally she forced her way into the pages of this book. I believe she has something more to say. And I have a question for her: How can she be the church if Vatican II is right and we are to understand the church as "the people of God"?

I only hope that I can get in my part of the conversation with you before she breaks in and takes over.

* * *

The source of all references and quotations in this book not explicitly mentioned in the text are in the *Works Cited,* pp. 216–222.

2

Adding Care to Justice

The absence of a trustworthy pattern of care for human beings and the environment has become all too familiar to us today. While unnecessary new shopping centers provide momentary distractions for middle-class suburbanites, city dwellers are reminded every day that racism, drugs, family violence, abandoned neighborhoods and homelessness affect everyone.

Until we acknowledge the pervasiveness of these conditions, we aren't even ready to ask what we can do about them. After working with many women just awakening to their responsibility in regard to such broad policy issues, I am convinced that such awakening, combined with the vision offered by some women artists and scholars, suggests a transformative approach to these problems.

As I listen to what my students are saying these days, particularly mothers returning to school after years at home, I am startled into the sense that our society is at a critical in-between time. Our county, for instance, has "good" schools, relative prosperity, and talented, generous people, but these adult students are beginning to realize the thinness of the "good life" they hoped to find in the suburbs and to wonder about what kind of values they are passing on to their children. Like my younger students, they are beginning to suspect that neither politicians, experts nor religious leaders know how to control the forces that are responsible for drugs, crime and homelessness, that arm nation against nation, and that even threaten the life of the oceans and earth itself.

But to sum up these realities in easy generalizations is almost to deny the crucible of experience which has raised such doubts. Many hitherto homebound mothers used to be almost totally absorbed in trying to bring up good healthy children. Today they are forced to raise fundamental questions about the world into which they are introducing them.

One class in particular brought this home to me. It was in a course called "People in Families," with a rich mix of age and background among the students. On this day, seventeen year old Kim presented an oral report on her earlier experience with drugs. She told us how she had yielded to pressure from her friends—"I was afraid I'd lose them otherwise"—and gone through a rebellious period in which she accused her parents of not understanding her. When her father and mother felt they could no longer handle her, they sent her—at fifteen—to a special boarding school where she had been living for two years. Kim told us the painful story with remarkable objectivity, showing considerable understanding of her family's behavior, and announcing that she was going home for a visit the following weekend.

Before her report, the class had tended to separate itself into two conversational groups, the young and the old. That day it became one. Kim's willingness to share something so intimate with them, and to accept a share of responsibility in her family's dilemma, touched the older students. They thanked her and reassured her that she would do well at home.

When the class ended most of the students left

quickly, but four mothers in their mid-thirties stayed on, continuing to react to Kim's report. At first the talk was general. Then Ann revealed that she had recently discovered her own twelve year old daughter used drugs. She had not felt able to bring it up before outside the family. But in this sympathetic group of mothers with equally unmentionable problems—one with an alcoholic husband, another with resentful stepchildren—Ann could at last talk about what concerned her most instead of holding it all in. Kim's story had made her realize that her use of drugs was not simply her own failure or her daughter's; she could not put all the blame on her child's friends or even on those selling the drugs. It had to be spread around. I could hear Ann and the others begin to make connections between the problems their children faced every day and the wider forces of society, that network of powerful but largely invisible forces that anthropologists call "culture."

Most of the students in the class had a hard time arranging their tight schedules so they could spend a few hours at college. The majority of those who were mothers juggled work outside the home, housework and their children to get to class, and were disturbed to realize how many of their children found school boring. After a long silence, Ann raised a question that had been simmering below the surface of their thoughts: "Why does what's good seem so dull and uninteresting to our kids, when what hurts them seems so powerful and attractive?"

Many of these women had struggled to make it from the Bronx or Brooklyn of their childhood to the green oasis our county seemed to offer. Yet here were the same problems they thought they had left behind, and there were no easy explanations. They looked at each other searchingly as if to say, "We've taken too much for granted, depended too much on what others told us. Maybe *we* have to do something."

The reason I can interpret what my students were going through is because I have gone through the same process. In the turbulent 1960s, just before the explosion of the contemporary women's movement, I felt a similar sense of inadequacy as a stay-at-home mother of four sons. Very little that I had been taught by my parents, my mostly good schools, or my church turned out to be much help in guiding my own children in a world that I was unprepared for. Instead of the loving and giving I had been told were the primary motherly virtues, I needed sound observational skills, the basic ability to translate and negotiate, the confidence and courage to speak up and sometimes to challenge authority—all areas in which I had not been trained. I, too, turned to other women for information and support, wondering if the rather abstract, passive ideals of motherhood encouraged by the church had left them in similar straits.

First I talked to friends, then I wrote to people I knew, and finally I developed a series of questions incorporating the range of the issues they raised in a survey that I distributed around the country in 1965. I was astounded by the length and intensity of the hundreds of responses I received to what had by then become a long questionnaire. Single women, wives and mothers—all seemed to be reexamining their lives and finding out that the rules they had been taught and the roles they had been assigned were no longer adequate to the reality they faced, whether in households, at work, or in convents.

The audience I heard from was largely Christian; the majority were Catholics. I had been inclined to accept Simone de Beauvoir's contention that Catholic women accepted the stereotypical roles assigned to women because

they had been subjected to a double dose of indoctrina-
tion; perhaps her point was valid in France, but the response I got indicated something quite different. This may
have been because the mid-1960s were a special time for
Catholics in general and women in particular, an interim
period just after the Second Vatican Council and before
the pope dismissed his own birth control commission because its members believed contraception could be compatible with church tradition and thinking. American
ideas of equality were helping these women criticize their
unequal place in the church, while their faith in God and
strong belief in justice, stimulated by church teaching,
had sharpened their ability to criticize American individualism. I gave voice to some of these women in *Sex: Female; Religion: Catholic,* aware that more was going on in
their lives than they or I could then capture in words: new
thinking, wrenching personal transformation, decisions to
renegotiate and sometimes break marriage contracts, to
leave religious orders, to create new vocations.

Men responded to my survey too, and often they
agreed with the women. It is instructive to look back
twenty-five years and see that the vast majority of those
men and women thought it proper for both parents to take
on roles that were usually assigned by gender. They believed that fathers should nurture and mothers should educate, continue their own education, and work outside the
home. But the language and passion of the women who
replied made me realize that something more powerful
than intellectual agreement lay behind their words. The
dominant note in their responses was clearly an attach-
ment to other human beings as equals deserving care—a
traditional religious concern, you might say. Whatever
their disagreements, and there were many, they were all
raising disturbing questions. Some were local: "Why

should our parish redecorate the church when there are homeless people in town?" Others were global: "When will the church realize that it's responsible for everyone on this globe and not just for its own institutions?"

Years later, when I read Carol Gilligan's study of women's development, *In a Different Voice,* I assented immediately to her discovery that relationship to others was central to women's sense of identity and moral reasoning. This was clearly what lay behind the emphasis on caring that was so dominant in my survey responses. What was especially interesting to me, however, was that the majority of the women who had filled out my questionnaire did not express their concern for such care in terms of the old stereotypes that said women were "by nature" more involved with their hearts than their heads. Instead, they were using their heads along with their hearts to reveal the inadequacy of such clichés. Like the connected knowers that women psychologists have discovered mature women thinkers to be, they thought about what they cared about and cared about how they thought.

The women I heard from in 1965 were reshaping their ideas in response to the real conditions they faced, and this in turn forced them to reexamine their old assumptions. They were already learning to negotiate the stages of the life cycle, living out the implications of the theory developed by Erik Erikson and popularized by many others in the 1970s. In a journal she wrote in her eighties, Florida Maxwell-Smith summed up the process as many women experience it when she suggested that life is a long pregnancy in which we give birth to ourselves. Focusing on birth as a metaphor for human development was not usual, however, in the first wave of feminism. Many of its most vocal proponents were seeking freedom from motherhood as they struggled for greater control over their lives, the right not to marry or have children, and the opportunity to pursue any career that suited their talents and dreams. Because of disastrous personal experiences, some deeply resented and distrusted men in general. Others were outspoken opponents of childbirth: "Let scientists do it!" As usual, the media heightened and flattened their voices, creating a confrontational image of extremist feminists that could easily be played off against an image of equally extreme opponents posing as defenders of traditional values. Underneath this superficial clash of voices, however, an overall process of growth was taking place among millions of women who did not exactly fit into either camp.

Teaching those courses in contemporary mothering and people in families in the mid-1970s, I could sense the ambivalence that the majority of our students felt toward the early women's movement. "A counselor at the college told me she was glad I was finally going to do something with my life. As if I've been wasting my time caring for my six kids," one reported. "But it's certainly been more demanding than the secretarial job I used to have." In those days, college would give credit for demonstrated learning in earlier jobs such as dental assistant or a secretary, but never for years of mothering, even though it usually involved far more learning. Most of the mothers in those classes did not feel that their concerns were included in the feminism they heard about, even though they sympathized with many of its goals. They too were learning to trust their own observations and judgments and to acknowledge their own emotional needs, not just those of their children—indeed to see those needs as intimately related. And they were supporting each other in a group.

A few stories should suggest the flavor of what was happening there. Almost unconsciously, one Irish-American mother used class as a sounding-board to develop the strength to confront her Italian-American husband who had her doing secretarial work in "his" small business. By the end of the term she had talked herself into a lasting business partnership.

Another woman was tied up in knots by her inability to be an ideal mother. She came to class depressed: "I'm supposed to be serene no matter what happens but I can't do it." When she finally asked, "Do you mean it's OK to feel angry, even to feel you hate the kids sometimes?" everyone breathed easier. They knew by then that what mattered was what you do with those feelings, which you'd better accept and identify or they'll destroy you.

Many questions that were being discussed in feminist circles emerged spontaneously in these courses as a concern related to mothering. How much choice should women have in deciding to have children? How could medical practitioners and institutions become more tuned in to the natural and psychological aspects of birth? How could mothers find adult company and time away from their children? What could any of us do about developers spreading isolated homes all over the country, causing stores to move out of communities where they had previously given people natural places to meet?

When I meet some of the mothers from these classes on the street these days, they tell me things are getting worse. One who is now a grandmother shakes her head with a combination of sadness and anger and asks me, "Why doesn't anyone value mothering any more?"

I'd like to be able to answer her straight off, but like the mothers in my classroom after Kim's report, I have to wait and let it all sink in. I need to keep thinking, to find words that begin to describe what we have lost. I'm convinced that a clearer understanding of mothering is central to the attempt, but when I bring up the subject to a good friend who counsels women at the college, she gently tries to discourage me. "Do you think it's wise to talk about maternal values today? There's too much emphasis on self-sacrifice for women as it is. It's very hard for the women who come to me to plan lives that are good for them as well as for their husband and children."

Another old friend makes it clear she's equally suspicious of my project. A heavy dose of early idealization proved so destructive in her experience that she is allergic to the very word "mothering." So are some nuns I know, who still resent being told they were first and foremost "spiritual mothers." Even such friends are afraid that I'm trying to market motherhood under a new label, asking women to return to the home, reinforcing all the traditional scripts of church and society that insist women should live for others and find their fulfillment in having children.

My counselor-friend, like most psychologists, knows from both experience and theory that you cannot nurture others successfully unless you have a strong self. She regularly distributes copies of articles by Carol Gilligan on women's development. I have seen the life-giving power that information gives to adult women students, who xerox copies for their friends as if they were found treasure. They are just the ideas we need in public discussion. But my counselor-friend reminds me that things are getting worse for women despite all the publicity about the women's movement: women and children are the fastest-growing poverty groups, for instance, and rape is more widespread than ever. "Talk about parenting if you want to," she warns me, "but not about mothers. Maybe you can reach men."

Perhaps I'm stubborn, but unless we talk about mothering I don't believe we can ever understand and change the very conditions my friend is fighting. It's hard to talk about something new in old words that don't immediately become red flags, signals that start a charge or a retreat in an old battle. I want to talk about parenting and include men; many of the Vietnam veterans, firemen, and male second careerists in my classes have shown themselves just as concerned about children as mothers. More often they have bosses who are not, however. More than child rearing is involved; we are trying to deal with cultural habits that go much deeper, and the word "parenting" doesn't quite fit.

When I use "parenting" as a verbal Rorschach test, students spout abstract terms about the skills necessary to raise children. When I use "fathering," most say "breadwinner" or "disciplinarian." But when I use "mothering" the responses become intensely emotional and wildly contradictory—from "Just what I could use," and "Life's greatest joy," to "It's smothering me!" and "Impossible job!"

So I stick with "mothering," for in my experience such violent and opposed reactions force us either to probe further or to stop talking to one another. In class we argue and listen, and gradually most of us see that we have been talking about something much more complicated than we originally thought, when our own emotions and assumptions blocked the view. We sometimes come to realize that we agree on many things and even have common questions: Should the rest of us care if physical mothers and fathers don't or can't "mother" their children? Do single or professional people, or those long past the child-rearing age, have reason to be concerned about what happens to children not their own? Gradually we see that assumptions about motherhood and sex roles have much to do with our lack of a mothering community.

Anthropologist Mary Catherine Bateson insists that concern about children is crucial for all of us. She suggests that each adult should develop and maintain a relation with at least "one real flesh and blood child," because children need the support of many caring adults. Aunts and uncles used to function this way for a good many of us. But the grandmother I met on the street was right: it is much harder for parents to raise children today then it used to be. In our pressure-driven, me-first society, it has become difficult for couples to decide to have even one child. For many young couples today, a child poses a serious threat to careers—sometimes for both parents.

Bateson tells us that establishing a relationship with a child is as important for adults as it is for children, however. Only through personal contact with actual young people can adults place the daily decisions they make— what they buy, how they vote, how much energy they consume—in the proper context: how their decisions will affect the future. Many leaders and educators call for new thinking on those questions today, but most of what takes place in conference centers or gets printed in newspaper editorials is heavy with abstractions. A relationship with a child brings everything down to earth. When Bateson suggests that regular contacts with a living child should be central influences in the social and economic decisions we make, she is consciously extending the values engendered in a nurturing family to public life.

In a talk given to college students in November 1989, poet-novelist Alice Walker reinforces the advice that self-development requires a mothering attitude and behavior in a wider cultural and religious context:

> We grow and we change. That is our hope as human beings, and perhaps what we are all required to do is to adopt a Moslem child and raise it as Moslem. Or, in other words, to make a decision to choose someone totally unlike ourselves about whom to be concerned. And to support them wholeheartedly as they continue to be who they are.
>
> What other hope is there for our hate-filled world? A world in which everyone's children are imperilled.

An increasing number of women scholars and artists have begun to trace the connection between the absence of care in our culture and the continuing delegation of mothering almost entirely to mothers and to private life. Among them is poet Adrienne Rich, who believes it is vital for all women to explore their connection with women who bear children rather than escape from it. In *Of Woman Born* she says that the "unexamined assumptions" about mothers and motherhood pose the real problems. This mother of three sons explains how her early feelings of anger and entrapment changed to affirmation of the great resource that mothering could add to human life, helping to reconnect it with "the natural order, the corporeal ground of our intelligence."

Now that the whole earth is ravaged, only such integrative thinking, grounded in real physical contexts, can bring about the kind of transformed attitudes necessary to build a future. In her vision of the earth as holy icon, Brita Stendahl conveys our present situation with power and precision. Looking at a photograph of the earth taken from the moon she cries out:

> There she swims in dark blue space, our mother, our home, a jewel, shimmering, yet soft. There we live and must live together.
>
> Languages, traditions, religions, customs, costumes, color, creeds and sex have separated humankind. Here we have a picture of how we belong together. An image to replace the mighty image of Man drawn by Leonardo do Vinci, which has served so long as a symbol for our conquering civilization and which, not incidentally, inspired the creation of the astronauts and cosmonauts: Man as his own measure drawn within circles, being the center and reaching out with strong arms and legs to the periphery, the emblem that gave courage to Renaissance Man, the model for explorers, inventors, and hero of the humanists. The picture of Mother Earth humbles that image of Man and forces us into new languages of nourishment, care and survival, things that we formerly took for granted.

Recognizing this need to develop such new languages, a few women have begun to bring the deep, personal voices of their own childhood into their professional life and thought. Mary Catherine Bateson and Sara Lawrence Lightfoot have written important books about their extraordinary mothers, anthropologist Margaret Mead and child psychiatrist Margaret Lawrence. They also reveal how particular lives develop in ever-widening circles, so that the positive values nourished through family interchange can reach out to a society that craves them.

Both women are trained social scientists as were their pioneering mothers, able to describe their subjective experience objectively. Their lives and work help us see what can happen when women are respected as equals in marriage and work, and bring up their children with similar respect.

Bateson admits that it will take time for the "exciting and painful" changes that now affect child-bearing and marriage to percolate through the whole social fabric, shifting our ideas of what it is to be human. But she sees the process as essential if we are to build a community in which "different" does not mean inferior.

Sociologist Lightfoot, at the Harvard Graduate School of Education, has developed guidelines for educators at every level which foster this new language of respect for the "whole persons" who are their students. Help the silent ones to tell their stories, she advises, so that their voices can create a new public discourse which respects difference in all the particular, real contexts of life. Blending the language of social science with that of literature, Lightfoot insists that "only in the particular resides the general."

If we want to work realistically for justice in this world, we need to listen to such voices. I heard Sara Lightfoot deliver the words above in a conference we ran at our college called Our Stories/Ourselves, with storytellers and singers as well as psychologists. The written reactions from those who attended confirmed the power of family and ethnic storytelling in shaping identity and fostering relationships.

Mothers who attended wrote about its healing force. One who had been forced by her father to reject a scholarship elsewhere and attend our local college sixteen years ago reflected on the irony of coming back. Here she was in

the same place where, in defiance of her father's authority, she had wasted her time. Now she hopes she will provide a different example for her daughter.

The conference confirmed the importance of such
personal, familial decisions in ways that transcended the
usual separation of intellectual from overall human development. "Healing must be at the center of the educational
experience," Sara Lightfoot said. The mother above reported that by stressing family storytelling, the conference had been more therapeutic in healing family wounds
than any counseling session: "The wall of animosity between my mother and myself has started to crumble." A
single woman's reflection reveals the power of shared
storytelling to bridge even further divisions: "I took Professor Lightfoot's comment on healing to refer to personal
healing, which brings about group healing, and finally
community healing."

Such healing, which could go on in almost any daily
encounter, starts with the kind of awakening I observed
among mothers in my classes. It is fostered by all those
caring forces that build self-respect and encourage people
to tell their stories. This is the good mothering we all need
if we want to heal the communal and ecological wounds
from which we suffer today.

3

Should the Church
Be a Mother?

If mothering is a central need today for the earth and its people, surely a church that has long called itself a mother ought to be centrally involved in providing it. But there are many people, including lifelong Catholics, who either don't find the church credible as a mother, or can accept the image only in terms of some less endearing maternal characteristics. They emphasize the church's hierarchical structure: "Are you kidding?" they ask. "There are no women in positions of power; how can you call a church like that a mother?"

In an open discussion on the topic, I will surely hear several other people explain how this church or real mothers hurt them emotionally. "I just got away from a mother like that, and I don't intend to get involved with another." The topic looks hopelessly onesided, but wait—someone in the back is trying to say something. He's a little stiff at the start, but obviously speaks from deep conviction: "It's not a question of men and women or of our emotional problems. Tradition has always referred to the church as a mother because she's supported us by giving us the sacraments and preserving Christ's teaching."

Such disagreements may be painful but they provoke discussion that leads to new thinking. And in the metaphor of Mother Church we have a common image in which to ground our discussion, whether our emotional reaction is positive, negative, or neutral, as mine was at the start. Metaphors can hold different, even contradictory ideas together in fruitful tension. They allow us to air our differences and still keep talking to each other, and they are capable of doing even more. When a friend reported that she had seen the word "Metaphor" on a moving van in Greece—literally, the word means "to carry over"—it was an amusing reminder of the power of a metaphor like Mother Church to help us move our thinking as well. This is essential when we are seriously reappraising both terms, mother and church. In her searching commentary on the myths and metaphors governing contemporary American culture, Madonna Kolbenschlag says that part of our confusion is because we are caught between metaphors. This is certainly true of our mixed reaction to the image of Mother Church. It reflects emotionally-held differences of interpretation that may reveal even deeper sources of division than the shouting would indicate, yet still offer grounds for potential agreement.

The image of Mother Church is ancient, but it still springs naturally to the minds of many contemporary believers. Notice that it's a feminine image, but at the same time it represents all of us, men and women. It suggests that women, feminine values and feminine virtues have always been essential to the church, even if they are not visible in its institutional leadership. At the same time this metaphor needs reinterpretation because of what we now know about "mother" and "church" from contemporary psychology, recent history, and theology itself, because of our sounder understanding of gender differences and of mothering, and the official church's self-description as "people of God." Metaphors are not only moving vans; they can be two-way streets.

In my lifetime, the church's institutional leadership has sometimes given impressive indications of maternal vision. Younger readers, unfortunately, may find it hard to realize the sense of exhilaration many of us felt in the early 1960s as we waited for the next installment of the behind-the-scenes story of Vatican Council II to be served up by Xavier Rynne in *The New Yorker*. We felt a thrill of hope because Pope John XXIII insisted that the council be "pastoral" rather than "dogmatic," that the bishops concern themselves with the welfare and development of people, not with denouncing heresies or wringing hands at contemporary trends. A little later, John's encyclical letter *Peace on Earth*, written shortly before his death in 1963 and addressed to all the world's peoples, showed how broad his hopes had become. Here he sketched the outline of the world family living in a peaceable kingdom on earth, in which air and water would not be poisoned, animal species not decimated daily, and people not sacrificed to the devouring idols of nationalism, free enterprise, or progress.

Peace on Earth also pointed out that such harmony could not be mandated *for* others; people would have to be enabled and trusted to carry out their own plans, responsibly and cooperatively. This meant that poor and third world peoples as well as women must be free to determine their own lives "in the social and economic sphere, in the fields of learning and culture, and in public life."

Pope John's words were truly prophetic—issued, incidentally, in the same year that saw the publication of Betty Friedan's *The Feminine Mystique*. This elderly Italian cleric, sitting at the very top of the ecclesiastical power structure, already knew that if women did not rethink and reshape their own roles, neither the church nor the world could carry out the common task of building "the relationships of the human family in truth and justice, in love and freedom." In his eyes, we were all part of one creation, a potential sacrament revealing God's loving goodness. His was not the rational, bureaucratic mind that divides reality into sacred and secular, or assigns priests to the care of "souls," women to the care of children, and men to the care of the body politic. Aware of the top-heavy structure of the institutional church and of the way in which time-bound customs tend to take on the claims of tradition, John had called the council in order to let fresh air into the church.

For John the church existed not to serve itself, but the promptings of the Spirit. It was clear to him that Rome could not speak in accordance with the Spirit until it did a lot more listening. To begin with, there had to be a consultation with bishops—who in turn were to consult their people—of every race, from every continent. Although for many Vatican bureaucrats and others this process seemed radical—"the church already has the answers"— or even dangerous, it was in fact a time-honored approach because questions change from one generation to the next. In the late nineteenth century, John Cardinal Newman wrote that consulting the faithful on matters of faith was the traditional way to determine authentic Christian teaching. He supported his position with an intensive historical review of the practice of the church in the fifth century.

Today, however, the Vatican seems to be shutting its windows. After years of fruitful consultation among different national hierarchies in the spirit of Vatican II, most notably in the Latin and North American churches, Rome has adopted a more defensive stance. In contrast, before issuing their recent pastoral letters on nuclear weapons and the American economy, U.S. bishops carried on lengthy and broad-based consultation with the faithful; perhaps that is why these documents caught the attention of the wider public. This practice of good listening has continued on other subjects, but there is increasing pressure to abandon this approach—which will never produce results that will please everybody and therefore always leaves some bruises—as the fear that the laity might be "confused" seems to have replaced the spirit of mutual trust.

The same pattern is often seen in families when the parents are afraid for their children. Except for the very young, however, who still need to be carried, it does not work. Listening is of the greatest importance when there are disagreements, and adult Christians need to understand the reasoning behind basic church decisions. Disagreements in the church are largely differences of opinion among adults based on their different experience. The problem is magnified if one group denies the importance of experience while the other considers it essential to meaning. Such stances reflect such profound divisions of understanding about the inclusiveness of the church, and whether or not it is more than its structures of authority, that unless conversation is fostered, the church family itself is in danger of falling apart.

Let me make a few simple observations on what is implied by this tug-of-war that now exists in the church. Last week I heard a sermon in which a pleasant young priest explained to the congregation the difference between parochial and public schools. "We tell the children who they are, what they have to do, and where they're going," he said confidently; "they never have to doubt or worry."

Young people surely need ideals, a sense of direction, and limits on their behavior, but I fear that the attitude of that priest has a great deal to do with why so many of the eighteen year olds I meet in college who have been to parochial school or attended after-school classes in church doctrine think that their religion asks nothing of their minds. They see it as something already complete, in which their role is simply passive; it has been mediated to them by authorities who simply insist that they behave in a certain way. It is unlikely that such an approach will reach them on a personal level. First, because elements of this teaching are uncongenial to a majority of young Americans today. And second, because little effort has been made to involve them in its articulation, to help them see that some of it might correspond to their deepest desires. In the face of our consumer culture Christian ideals of peace and justice will appeal only to a dedicated minority. For most, however, a heavy emphasis on negative prohibitions and strict authority seems to overshadow the vague encouragement to love their neighbors and follow a largely unreal figure called Jesus.

This puts teenagers—especially the most thoughtful among them—in a dilemma. Either they remain faithful by following such advice, or they decide to trust their own minds and experience. In the latter case, they are all too apt to come to believe, like Huckleberry Finn, that the morality they actually develop through observation and reflection is somehow at odds with the faith their parents hoped to pass on. They often end up thinking that they are leaving their faith behind at precisely the point when for the first time they are accepting an adult responsibility for

it. They may have been brought to mass since they were
infants, but in how many parishes would they have been
made aware of the powerful strand of church thinking expressed by Karl Rahner when he said that the religious
obligation of the present was to become "free, creative
persons"? Probably the greatest Catholic theologian of
the century, he continued till the end of his life to insist
that we seek and serve God precisely through the experience of daily life.

Such an approach is reinforced by the witness of our
most admired spiritual guides, who seem equally unex-
plored in most Catholic education. Even an introductory
acquaintance with Teresa of Avila or a contemporary like
Thomas Merton would reveal their insistence on the interaction between our personal encounter with God and the
way we behave to other people. Their awareness that to
some extent we create ourselves and our world is reminis-
cent of the medieval concept—conveyed so powerfully to
me in the work of Etienne Gilson when I was in college—
of our responsibility to discover the idea of our being in
God's mind, as Aquinas might have put it. Both St. Teresa
and St. John of the Cross insist that self-knowledge and
self-discipline are essential to seeing and sharing in God's
love in all the circumstances and relationships of daily
living.

To achieve the self-discipline that springs from encounter with life requires a continuing self-education
which involves reflection and results in action: "I saw him
and I sought him," said the fifteenth century English mystic Julian of Norwich. Except for the late medieval religious vocabulary, she could be talking about what a modern developmental psychologist like Erikson or an
educator like Piaget would call human maturation. But Julian, though brilliantly analytical, preferred to talk in the

language of metaphor. The God she discovered as the fruit of her maturation could only be described in maternal terms, as in the following excerpt from *Showings:*

> This fair lovely word "mother" is so sweet and so kind in itself that it cannot truly be said of anyone or to anyone except of him and to him who is the true Mother of life and of all things. To the property of motherhood belong nature, love, wisdom and knowledge, and this is God.

Most young people I know have not been led to draw on such resources; they received only the well-intentioned formulas the young priest in my parish proudly offered as praise for parochial schools. They can arrive at college without ever having encountered someone who spoke in the name of religion and asked them to integrate their faith with their growing sense of self, their increased ability to think things out, and their often contradictory attitudes to others. Of course, the majority of them are likable and represent a tremendous potential for good; quite a few care about the homeless and are angry about ecological abuse and waste. Some even have the energy and dedication to try to change things. But very, very few have the least awareness that knowing more about sociology, psychology, economics, literature or science is at the heart of their vocation as students and could serve to illuminate their spiritual lives as well as their careers. Nothing in their previous experience seems to suggest to them that the church could help their thinking through its witness to detachment, to truth-seeking for its own sake, or to the exposure of self-delusion and hypocrisy. Apparently they have not experienced such witness.

Is it surprising then that when I meet with parents

who were actively involved with church groups that helped prepare millions for the changes that were given authoritative endorsement at Vatican II, I so often hear them repeating the same lament: "Our children don't seem to be involved with the church the way we used to be." Their children are "leaving the church," or perhaps just sitting on the sidelines; others are joining smaller, more emotionally-oriented religious groups outside Catholicism, or getting involved in justice causes, indicating their concern for human community.

One mother put it this way: "I don't think the church has any impact on my children. I'm afraid they only go to church because I bring them. This makes me sad. How will they cope with things when they develop their cynical eye, when they begin to question things, as I have? I continue to go to mass with the hope that somehow a change will take place; I can stay in the church because I've managed to work out my own understanding of religion. But the middle stages of life will inevitably bring crises and difficulties; that is when we all need something to hold onto. What will my children do then?"

Like so many parents, she has learned that it is impossible simply to tell children who they are, what they should do, and where they are going—except perhaps when they are very young. Even then it will not help them very much; it will not become *their* understanding unless it matches their reflection on their own experience. As they grow, they will inevitably test what they have learned from family, school and church against all they are learning from friends, popular music, work, higher education and life itself. If their experience of "church" does not encourage them to make those connections, to have confidence in themselves as they learn from their mistakes, and to share their experience within the church community, such a formation will at most leave them with a one-sided, privatized spiritual life. Because there is such powerful pressure from the wider culture to be "winners," this turn to a purely private faith is a frequent choice for young people trying to be faithful to what they have received but without the resources to integrate it wholly into their everyday lives. It is hardly surprising—but ought to be somewhat disturbing—that, according to a recent report in *The New York Times,* Roman Catholic seminarians today "conceive of their work in terms of celebrating the sacraments, preaching and working with individuals, rather than building up a community, cooperating with lay staff or carrying out administrative tasks." In most parishes I have visited the priests operate on a similar interpretation of their mission.

The church could be different and truer to its ancient communal traditions. The problem is: When we are so divided, how can we bring into existence a more communal church? How can we learn to work with one another toward such a goal? Perhaps we can catch a glimpse of what might be possible by listening to reflective adult believers such as sociologist and long-time peace-builder Elise Boulding, who shares a retrospective look at the processes in her early life which helped her to develop an inner life that demanded the outer attempt to build community.

"As a very small child," she tells us, "I had a vivid sense of the connectedness of heaven and earth." Every Christmas her parents walked her slowly around the starlit tree, holding her hand and telling her stories of the great king from heaven who came down to earth as a baby every year:

> I have a distinct image of Jesus the king, sitting by an open window in his castle in the heavens, lis-

tening to the prayers of children from earth in the
long stretches of months between Christmases.
The sky never felt distant, but near. Heaven was
roomy and full of love. This made me feel very
secure at night. I loved the dark because I could
feel heaven. I could feel the stars, too, even when
the night sky was overcast and they could not be
seen.

Boulding goes on to say that because she could imagine that heavenly castle in her mind, she knew it was also
inside her. In this way the foundation was laid for her to
welcome all new information, including the scientific discoveries of the twentieth century, so often unsettling for
those unable to integrate faith and experience. She could
have confidence that God's work and ways were infinitely
mysterious and that his kingdom was nevertheless within
her, asking her to appreciate them. Boulding learned
through the power of her imagination, in response to her
parents' stories, to trust both the world and her response
to it.

The foundation of such a trusting, imaginative response can be reported in stories but the words and stories
themselves come from deeper sources. In his spiritual
journal *Morning Light* priest-novelist Jean Sulivan relates
that after the death of his mother he detached himself
from "all the folklore of religion" and became a wanderer
"in the desert of cities." He resolved "to keep as far away
as possible from the whole pious circus":

But the first words of my mother, her voice, her
gestures and the swaying of her body had been
too strong. Her word came from the beginning of
time, and in the cursed and cherished city it

caught up with me. No longer able to walk on paths underneath the trees or along running streams, I let images of forests and water rise from my own depths, and suddenly there was a murmur: "Jerusalem, Jerusalem, how many times have I wanted to gather together your sons like a hen gathers together its chickens." I felt a certainty, even though my mind saw obstacles and absurdities everywhere. Agnosticism and skepticism remained intact in me. Nevertheless something was drawing me, a confidence in the night, like a gladness of the flesh which was perhaps not only flesh.

The kind of mothering that Boulding and Sulivan describe helped them respond freely and positively to *this* world, able to distinguish the Spirit that is visible everywhere to those who can see. Carol Ochs believes that such mothering is natural to those who care for very young children:

To mother is to love. . . . Loving a child does not mean sentimentally gushing over it—it means, first and foremost, physical caring. Loving a child means loving it for itself and not for what it can give to your own self. Mothering entails a species of empathetic, prelinguistic knowledge: to understand an infant is to understand without verbal cues. It is learning to let go; the total involvement that is so essential for an infant would be obtrusive for a toddler. In short, mothering means decentering the ego—for a while the child must come first.

What might such mothering mean throughout the church today when so many of its "children" are in fact adults? Reexamining the image of Mother Church as it occurs in the formative years of the church can help us imagine an answer. The image appeared in the writings of the church fathers in the first three centuries, where it symbolized, surprisingly, not a powerful authority but the action of all its members. In *The New Catholic Encyclopedia* Carl Delahaye says that the image of Mother Church conveyed "the strong sense that the fathers had of the entire church body as one communion of all the faithful in Christ." He goes on to assert that the image emphasizes "the responsibility of all the faithful for all others in the life of the community, their effective and genuine participation, their authentic and living collaboration in the duties of the community in the midst of this world." Because the church is "the great We of the faithful in Christ and in his Spirit," all together are enabled and required to serve in unison the handing on of this common faith and tradition.

Many may be as astonished as I was to find such a vision of spirit-filled equality in the vision of the early fathers. Yet it is in complete harmony with St. Paul's image of the church as the body of Christ that has been presented to us since childhood, perhaps without much reflection on its implications. Indeed it is simply another way of pointing to a similar vision, never capable of clear and complete expression. And, of course, it strongly echoes the notion of the communion of saints, the interrelationship through space and time of all those who are united in Christ.

When it is informed with a sense of good mothering, this image of Mother Church seems pertinent as a contemporary ideal because is capable of mediating the sense of human solidarity we badly need to develop. A memory from the childhood of Christianity, it is strikingly similar to the ideal toward which Vatican II was moving in its attempts to decentralize authority and bring together bishops from Africa, Asia, and Latin America, as well as Europe and North America, along with Orthodox and Protestant observers. If church leaders were really prepared to listen to and consult all those who raise their voices today, and abandon unreal hopes of returning to an idealized middle ages or to the 1917 Code of Canon Law, we might be able to reconnect with the earlier, broader tradition that the image of Mother Church ultimately represents.

Far more than when Pope John XXIII first pointed out the need to hear them, it is the voices of women that especially need a hearing in the church. But they are often interpreted—as it appears Pope John Paul II apparently interpreted the polite but firm voice of Sister Teresa Kane —as voices of opposition, threats to authority, rebels who want to overthrow the divinely mandated rule of men. Such a picture fits easily into the framework of popular journalism, because it offers a public image of dramatic conflict. As I hear them, however, these women are actually offering constructive insights on common problems. Many are well prepared to share with the church community the hard-earned fruits of their own experience. They may have passed through moments of awakening and anger, but most have achieved new patience. They are "hanging in," hoping for a new openness in the church community, but continuing to grow and serve wherever they can.

The voices of these women, even though they may seem unimportant and even troubling to many in power, are actually a reminder of the humanity of the whole church. When they share their experience, it reminds us of all the rich, diverse material we must integrate within ourselves if we are to grow in self-understanding. In the last twenty years, many women have shared their experiences of growth publicly with the broader community. Included but not consulted, they have had to struggle to achieve mature identities as believers and human beings. This is the very process that present challenges require of all of us, men and women, especially from those who understand that the incarnation is not just an abstract dogma, but a clear indication of the responsibility of believers. Listening to women, then, we can learn how to accept and deal with a world groaning for fulfillment. As Madonna Kolbenschlag says, reflecting on the needs of contemporary humanity, "Everyman today is a woman."

What I am pointing to can probably best be illustrated by looking at the contributions of a few representative, though uniquely gifted, women. Mary Gordon's richly comic novel *The Company of Women* shows us what it was like to grow up female and Catholic in the old-fashioned church when "Father" laid down the law, and then come of age in the "liberated" 1960s. She tells the story of Felicitas, brought up in a circle of women who give unwavering support and admiration to their spiritual director, Father Cyprian. The latter takes great interest in the girl's education and is especially concerned to make it intellectually strong, rooted in objective truth.

One day when the sensual, aesthetically responsive girl reveals her tendency to love the world's beauty by praising the smell of grass, the priest reprimands her in this satirically heightened but telling admonition:

> . . . . you must not be womanish. It was womanish to say, "How sweet the grasses are." It was womanish to say the rosary during mass. It was womanish to carry pastel holy cards and stitched

novena booklets bound with rubber bands. It was womanish to believe in happiness on earth, to be a Democrat, to care to be spoken to in a particular tone of voice, to dislike curses, whiskey and the smell of sweat. Vigil lights were womanish, and spiritual chain letters, *The Catholic Digest, The Sacred Heart Messenger,* statues of the Infant of Prague that could be dressed in different colors for the different liturgical seasons.

The opposite of womanish was orthodox. The Passion of Christ was orthodox, the rosary said in private (it was most orthodox to prefer the sorrowful mysteries), the Stations of the Cross, devotion to the Holy Ghost, responding to the mass in Latin, litanies of the Blessed Virgin and the saints. Tower of ivory, house of gold, Ark of the Covenant, gate of heaven, morning star. To love these words was to know God. To love the grasses was to be in error. Error has no rights, said Father Cyprian, explaining why it was that outside the Church there was no salvation.

With such training, Felicitas all too predictably falls prey to an egotistical professor who persuades her that sexual liberation is a fuller expression of her belief in the natural. But the beauty and power of "the company of women" in which she had been formed are not so easily forgotten, especially as she comes to recognize the emptiness of so much of contemporary culture. When she finds herself pregnant, Felicitas simply cannot go through with an abortion, and the end of the narrative finds her returning with her baby girl to the circle of Father Cyprian's admirers, where relationships have changed dramatically.

In different ways, for different reasons, both Felicitas

and Father Cyprian have arrived at a genuine appreciation of ordinary human virtue. Both have reevaluated the unpretentious, humble care that the women have given the priest, and come to realize that such love is stronger and more enduring than his earlier prideful brilliance. Father Cyprian shows that he has learned that it is his regular contact with these women—this man who had always talked against "womanish" things—that has brought him back to life. "I am doomed," he says, "like the rest of my kind to the terrible ringed accident of human love."

Some will say that a novel is only one artist's shaping of reality; it is true that such a vision is inevitably selective. But to me this comic version of one Catholic woman's education-through-life seems to capture the maturing process of women in general, and to suggest its healthy possibilities for church and culture. Mary Gordon has succeeded in the difficult task of describing the gradual stages through which a young woman forms a stable identity. Felicitas is not just a Catholic, a woman, or an American. She is pulled this way and that by elements in all these identities before she gets to know her own taste and talents. Rushing headlong into life from the cloistered precincts of Father Cyprian's orthodoxy, she gradually learns who and where she is. And it is through the example of Felicitas that the priest comes to discover his own humanity. Previously he had thought that his identity lay exclusively in his splendid, masculine understanding of priesthood; now he recognizes the privilege he has in being able to play with Felicitas' happy little daughter.

It is this process of needing to reflect and become whole people in relationship with one another that we find again and again in contemporary women's testimonies. Believers or non-believers, Italian-Americans or Latin-Americans, bishops or bartenders, business women or housewives, we are all fragmented, sometimes not even seeing the need to unite these pieces of self. Yes, we have made strides in overcoming ethnic exclusivism since the days of my childhood, when Irish, Polish and Italian Catholics rarely mixed with one another, and marriages between them were called "mixed." But though we have broadened our affiliations to the universal church and stretched our support to ecumenical action, it seems to me that all of us in the church still need to forge a human identity that is deeper and wider than the one we now inhabit so uneasily.

Elisabeth Schüssler-Fiorenza gives us another example of how to bring together seemingly divided pieces of self—in her case, those of committed feminist and biblical scholar. She has brought the early church closer to us by faithfully uniting both callings in her life and work. *In Memory of Her* patiently reconstructs the circle of followers around Jesus, the male and female friends whom he treated as equals. Her book also establishes the centrality of women in the church in apostolic times, carefully analyzing New Testament texts within the Jewish, Greek and Roman contexts in which Christianity arose. Happily, she has made the church more credible to today's women by rediscovering women's importance to the early church. In so doing, she has recovered an older tradition for all of us because she does not separate or idealize women, but recognizes that they, too, have sometimes exploited others from privileged positions within an overall patriarchy. If church officials began to adopt Greek and Roman patriarchal norms in order to gain support in the imperial culture, many women accepted them and some profited from them as well. That is why Schüssler-Fiorenza sees women's cause as identical with that of all who are poor, oppressed or powerless. Her vision of the church sounds like an up-to-date version of the ancient maternal image of the fathers: a place in which she told Annie Milhaven, "everybody can be included with their rights, their say, their vision and their decision-making. . . . In terms of theology, everybody has a gift from the Spirit and ought to participate."

Not only scholars, of course, point to the presence of the Spirit; so do mothers. In *Motherhood and God* British theologian Margaret Hebblethwaite reflects on how bearing and raising children today tunes us in to those motherly qualities of the creator that we have obscured for centuries. She reminds us of how hard it is for a young mother to survive with several energetic, battling children, even when she really wants them and has no outside job. But when this mother calls out for help and gets it, she is then able to share with others the God she has discovered:

> My God . . . is the one God to whom we all pray, and the truth of her love discovered in all the exhilarating and frustrating details of my motherhood is a truth that can be found by everyone, female or not, because God's love is truth and it is a love for all. . . . All comfort that comes from us, all creativity that breaks out from us, all tenderness that flows from us, comes ultimately from one source—our one, true and eternal mother, who is our God.

Of course it is not only women whose voices call on all the people of the church to stretch and deepen their identity, helping each other to grow. Benedictine Brother David Steindl-Rast insists on its spiritual necessity:

> We must all mother each other, whether we are men or women. . . . The one thing that is cer-

tainly true . . . is that *personhood,* what we have
made of ourselves in becoming somebody, is
something that will never be lost; but that is a
different thing from individuality. . . . And growing means to die to what we are in order to become what we are not yet. The seed has to die to
become a plant, and we have to die to being children in order to become adolescents, and so on.
But our most important death has to do with dying to our independence, as individuals, and so
coming to life as persons in our interdependence.

This is asceticism in the spirit of Vatican II, a deepening of identity in response to the reality and mystery of this
world. It implies a shuffling off of old scales, a burning off
of the fog of assumptions and stereotypes that limit our
receptivity to the world through which the Spirit tries to
reach us.

One of the messages I have heard that most cries out
for response comes from *Tell Me a Riddle,* Tillie Olsen's
story of a vision that came to her own mother just before
she died. A Jewish immigrant, she had passionately rejected official religion because in her native Russia it had
seemed part of her people's oppression. Just before her
death, however, Olsen's mother had a dream in which
someone knocked on her bedroom door. She smelled a
marvelous smell, heard a neighing sound, and saw three
wise men in gold, blue and crimson robes, embroidered as
in her old village. "We've come to talk to you," the first
one said. When she replied, "I'm not a believer," he assured her, "We don't want to talk about that. We want to
talk about wisdom."

"Come in," said the dying woman. Then she saw that
they were really women, not men, peasant women as in

the old country. They were worn out, but they had come, they said, to worship a universal human infant who was going to be crucified into divisions of sex, race and class. In her dream, shortly before she died, Olsen's mother joined them in this worship.

Although she had fiercely rejected all religious observances, this mother points to the deepest levels of spiritual community shared by all human beings. She reminds us too of God's maternal presence among the poorest of the poor. If we who consider ourselves believers could join her in this worship, then each mass, each communion would see us leave the church afterward with a full sense of the connection between all the experiences of our lives. Strong in the awareness of our own personhood and dedicated to the elimination of the multiple crucifixions that others undergo, we would be continuing the work of the Spirit that led John XXIII to call for the Second Vatican Council. We would also be on our way to realizing in contemporary terms the ancient vision of a church that knew how to be a good mother in this world.

4

Mothering in Symbol
and Human Need

If we all need to give and receive mothering, we'd
better be clear about what good mothering includes. The
answer is by no means obvious; the clichés that immediately spring to mind, whether sentimental or cynical, tend
to prevent our thinking clearly about both its human and
its divine aspects. There is no point in trying to establish a
scientific definition of mothering, but I have found useful
clues in recurring symbols in the history of art as well as
from the contemporary psychology of human development. These clues suggest some basic criteria for good
mothering and underlie the analysis that will follow in
later chapters.

Pre-historic, medieval and modern art reveals a striking continuity in human needs over the centuries: we want
to be assured that the universe is trustworthy, that we
have a function in it, and that the inevitable change and
death we face are not the ultimate meaning of our lives.
Ever since men and women have dwelt on earth, they have
seen nature as a mask of the forces of creation; whatever
name they have given to the source of nature, this meaning has been conveyed through maternal symbols of reassuring power.

The earliest known sculptures—from Spain to Siberia and throughout the Near East—are representations of female bodies, small, portable reminders of the feminine aspects of divine energy. In *The Masks of God* Joseph Campbell says that they were believed to give psychological support to women in childbirth, to support crops, homes and their occupants from danger, and to support the mind in its meditations on the mystery of being.

Men and women alike, in pre-historic and early agricultural societies, could find meaning in their existence through the natural changes of day into night, summer into winter, seed into corn, and life into death; feminine powers of renewal were seen as a reflection of divine energy. Central to these feminine powers was mother-power, the ability to give life out of one's body. Through pregnancy and birth, maternity represented the natural human ability to renew life despite decay and death. Motherhood symbolized divine fecundity and continuing presence despite change, with birth a model for all life transitions.

One symbol of the Mother Goddess is especially revealing of this essence of maternal force, its "holding" power—the goddess throne. Here the goddess is a woman whose lap, unnaturally extended, becomes a chair. She is literally the seat of life and growth, providing her devotees with the secure foundation they need in all their explorations and returns. Many such woman-chair sculptures exist, all of which represent the Great Mother, "seat" of the human race. According to psychologist Erich Neumann, she is the original form both of the goddess and of the throne itself, which represents the woman's motherliness not only in her womb but in her lap on which the newborn child is enthroned. The greatest such figure of the early cults was Isis, whose name itself means "seat" or "throne."

Most of us who shop at supermarkets might find it difficult to resonate to a grain goddess, but we can easily understand the need to be held. British child psychologist D.W. Winnicott originated the term "holding environment" to describe the kind of space that fosters an infant's growth. It allows a baby to explore enough to discover that it and mother are not one but two. After this discovery, however, the mother has to stay around to allay the infant's fears of separation. She must not over-protect, but should continue to care in a less obtrusive manner, so that the child can reincorporate her into a new sense of self. Such a space permits freedom within relationships and encourages the unpredictable, and to some extent given personality of the child to emerge through its own trials and errors.

Educational psychologist Robert Kegan has extended the term "holding environment" to similar situations of support needed at every stage of the lifespan if the human person is to continue to evolve. Pulling together separate theories of human development, he sees the need for the developing person to separate from a number of situations of earlier "embeddedness" in order to build a new identity, to distinguish self from the other as social being, thinker, worker or believer. Such a process is not only a separation; it is the creation of meaning which is increasingly accurate about both self and other.

Over the centuries, when artists have tried to capture such holding environments, representing trust and meaning in the cosmos as well as care and compassion for individual human beings, they have chosen maternal symbols like that of the goddess-chair. Since art possesses the mys-

terious ability to create a space we can enter, it provides us
with access to an earlier culture's sense of the shape and
meaning of human existence in a world very different from
our own. The painter's or poet's skill at rendering that
vision lets us enter that space and see it from our own
perspective as well. Viewing maternal symbols from pre-
historic and medieval European art, we can see essential
aspects of mothering emerge and overlap with what psychology, literature and life reveal. Taken together, they
suggest four essential aspects of the good mothering that
can provide such holding through life: nurturing, enabling, enduring and sharing.

     In all these cultural memories, men and women cher-
ish the presence of mothering and lament its absence.
Both attitudes are clearly illustrated in contemporary
African art. "Mother is Gold," says the Yoruban proverb.
In the art of the European middle ages, the protective,
nurturing aspect of mothering is most frequently and poi-
gnantly invoked in the figure of Mary with the infant Jesus
on her lap. Her contented child faces the world from this
perch with complete confidence, whether he has German,
Italian or Russian features.

     One of the best known and most beautiful renderings
of Mary as mother is found in the sculpture and the stained
glass windows of Chartres Cathedral, where in 1900
Henry Adams was overcome by his first vision of her
power. To understand why, it is best to go to the cathedral
and use his *Mont Saint Michel and Chartres* as a guide. If
that's not immediately possible, you can read about his
experience, which came to him with something of the
force that thrust St. Paul from his horse on the way to
Damascus. Adams was overpowered by the feminine di-

mension of God, the lost power of the feminine, which he wryly admitted he had never encountered in Massachusetts or Washington, D.C.

American men, he said, were not accustomed to feeling power emanating from a goddess; they felt it in machines and railroad engines. But on his first visit to Chartres, Adams met the force that earlier ages had experienced, and in *The Education of Henry Adams* he described it as "the greatest and most mysterious of all energies." Its absence at home made him feel alienated from the increasingly technological orientation of the United States in the late nineteenth and early twentieth century. It is sobering to recognize that, despite some feminist gains, the power of the machine over the imagination of American men has only increased since Adams' time, producing destructive military, ecological and social results.

Adams intuitively pointed to precisely those symbols of ultimate meaning that western idolization of progress had suppressed, though Europe's monuments, churches, and museums abound with images of this lost relationship. Completed in the thirteenth century, Chartres embodies meanings even older than itself. The time of its preeminence was perhaps the last in western history when religious symbols were strong enough to temper even royal power by providing a framework recalling an earlier unity with the natural world and its creatures, all held together by a compassionate creator. The vision of creative mercy embodied in such a cathedral unified and attracted pilgrims, rich and poor, in a way we isolated, end of the twentieth century individuals can hardly imagine. When we read Chaucer's *Canterbury Tales* we catch a glimpse of this vital world, where men and women of all types and classes could go on pilgrimage together to Canterbury Cathedral because they shared in the meaning that had built it, as did Chaucer himself.

Chartres, like so many other great churches built in honor of our Lady at that time, was erected above an earlier shrine to the Mother Goddess, the protector of women in childbirth, of crops, and of civilization itself. And the figure of Mary that recurs throughout the iconography of the cathedral is based on the earlier image of Isis holding her son Horus on her lap. In this way Mary brings the protective, nurturing function of the divine in pre-historic pagan times into the heart of Christian tradition. It is easy to understand how Mother Church could be seen as a powerful and comforting symbol in those days, because it reflected the common belief that creation could live in harmony with its creator. The ability of Christianity to endure for so many centuries is powerful evidence of the meaningful transaction between those symbols and the people's understanding of their everyday lives. These symbols both reflected and nourished meanings already present.

I have seen a triptych of Mary as mother by Nicolas Froment from fifteenth century Provence that is similarly reassuring in its presentation of divine compassion. The painting is kept locked up in the Cathedral of St. Savior in Aix-en-Provence. It is worth waiting in the dark while the sacristan fiddles with his keys and turns on the floodlights; the sudden revelation of style and content is overwhelming. Good King Rene and Queen Jeanne kneel in side panels in stunning red and black renaissance architectural settings. Surrounded by their favorite saints, they kneel and pray, facing the central panel which gives the work its name, "The Burning Bush." In this 1475 rendering of the Exodus text, a queenly mother is the central figure that mediates its meaning.

Moses is visible, of course, in the lower right fore-ground, related to the king and queen through the red of his rich robe. His sheep graze contentedly between him and the angel, who addresses Moses from the left fore-ground. The bush is a close-knit circle of green leaves, the merging crowns of a forest of trees rising above a rocky hilltop. Atop this plateau of leaves at the very center of the painting sits Mary, elegantly robed in dark satin, holding up her healthy baby who plays with a mirror, one of the symbols of the earlier mother-goddess. Beneath and around her, the circle of green treetops bursts into tongues of flame at their outer edges. As in the original text, nothing is consumed by this fire.

The artist has stunningly collapsed time and space, Old and New Testaments, to present Mary and her child as the long-awaited fruit of God's promise to the patriarch. He expresses the belief of his own time that God's cove-nant with the Israelites was fulfilled in the appearance of Mary and Jesus. Fifteenth century viewers could see themselves as heirs to this promise in their own landscape of recognizable castles, walled cities, fat flocks and rich colors. They could feel that they were descendants of Moses, Abraham and Sarah because the painting passes on the old tradition as it emerged within a medieval Euro-pean consciousness.

Mary's lap is one of the most consistent symbols of a holding environment in human history. By the time of Froment, however, western artists and believers had suffi-ciently distanced themselves from their embeddedness in nature to appropriate both it and Jewish history within their own rendition of contemporary Christian meaning. Yet the symbol of Mary's lap, like that of the goddess-chair, also speaks of the continuity of the human desire for secure mothering: natural, cultural and spiritual. As in the ancient world, people in the middle ages continued to relate maternal concerns to those of divinity.

So do our contemporaries. Memories of being held in their own mothers' laps, for example, are equally significant to nineteenth and twentieth century men and women. Novelist Henry James described his mother as the open yet enclosing lap of all the children's securities. She *was* each of them. Philosopher Sara Ruddick describes her own transformation of consciousness as deriving from a deep sense of loss at the absence of her mother's protection when she entered adolescence. As an adult she was divided between the professional thinking in her field and the intense emotional and interpersonal life she experienced at home as a wife and mother. Trying to heal the rift, Ruddick began to read Virginia Woolf and saw a common pattern in the way she and the novelist had been mothered.

It had been superb in the early protective stage. Woolf celebrated her mother as "the very centre of that great cathedral space that was childhood." Ruddick sums up Virginia's feeling of that space as "an impression of red and purple flowers which soon reveal themselves to be figures on a black background, her mother's lap in which young Virginia sat, on a train or bus, travelling in London . . . surrounded by beauty, both safely held and effectively moving." Ruddick observes that she, too, had been cared for with "exquisite competence" by a mother who had "created for me a childhood in which I was both held and safely moving, both secure and enabled."

Both had nevertheless been let down as adolescent girls when they badly needed enabling rather than protection. Woolf's mother died when she was thirteen, yet in the character of Mrs. Ramsay in *To the Lighthouse*, the novelist was able to create a classic portrait of the kind of mother who—all charm, intuition, and care for others—inevitably fails to provide for her daughter's enablement because of her own narrow ideology of womanhood. Ruddick recognized in this portrait the aspect of mothering she herself had lacked. Reflecting on its absence, she began to connect her thinking as mother and philosopher, enabling her to develop her theory of "maternal thinking."

Some may remember with gratitude having received the enabling that is the second aspect of mothering, but many more, like Woolf and Ruddick, must lament its absence. Fortunately, there are some North American symbols of the compassionate strength which the young and the weak need to find in the surrounding culture if they are to transform themselves into adults. The Statue of Liberty, holding high her torch, welcomes, illuminates, and makes room. In psychological terminology she corresponds to Erikson's adult virtue of "generativity," the ability to care for others lovingly. The statue represents well the enabling aspect of mothering, not only reaching out to individuals but mediating our country's most cherished ideals as the mother of exiles and refugees.

Medieval art had such a symbol as well. It is the traditional pose of the Mother of Mercy, sheltering kings, queens, and popes, but also poor friars, ordinary laborers and housewives under her generous mantle. Whatever their social position, all are covered by this gracious environment. Of course, this powerful image also functioned as the benevolent face of a too-powerful church that kept its members under strict control. Its central emphasis on mercy, however, and the equality of treatment given to the clearly adult and even high-ranking figures under her robe also suggests the genuinely powerful mother who can both "let go" and also remain in relationship with her adult children. Such a mother—and church—trusts her children to be independent, knowing that the relationship between them must constantly change if all are to grow and form new communities.

This second, enabling aspect of mothering can also be found in other examples of late medieval and renaissance art. Another remarkable painting from fifteenth century Provence, Enguerrand Quarton's "Coronation of the Virgin," depicts the scene of Mary's coronation in heaven in brilliant reds, blues and gold on an enormous canvas representing the entire geographical-theological universe of the time. It focuses on the same process Dante does in *The Divine Comedy,* the way in which God's mercy aids humanity in its ascent to heaven. A queenly Mary with long red hair is centered between, though slightly below, two handsome, similarly red-haired, identical young men, reflecting the theological point that the Father is known only through the Son. A hand of each places the crown on Mary's head, while the Holy Spirit soars above, a white dove whose wings stretch from the mouth of the Father to the mouth of the Son.

These four figures dominate the sky, also peopled by choirs of blue and red angels ranked in order and accompanied by kneeling saints. Mary's blue robe sweeps down from heaven to mingle with the sky below. An earth with recognizable local mountains and walled cites reaches up to touch the border of her robe, whose whiteness merges into the clouds. Directly below the center of Mary's robe, Jesus still hangs on the cross rooted in the earth. Visually as well as theologically, it is the only way to heaven. Below the cross on the left, an angel assists souls to emerge from purgatory and ascend the hill leading to the crucifix. On the lower right side, souls burn in hell, closed off from all exit. As in Dante, secular and ecclesiastical rulers inhabit both places.

Despite the physical positioning of heaven above earth in this universe, the artist shows a bold confidence that both are in constant touch—that the commerce between them is as regular as remembrance, prayer, a good deed, care of the garden or children, and everyday work. As the mother of the adult redeemer, Mary reminds us here that just as God is merciful, merciful love is the source of life, its inner meaning, a model for our behavior to one another.

Late classical Greek civilization celebrated similar enabling functions of mothering in its reverence for Demeter, the goddess of grain, who lost her daughter Persephone to the god of Hades, or death. While Demeter lamented for her daughter, the grain died. After a long, arduous search and much suffering and beseeching of Zeus to restore her daughter, however, Persephone was returned for half the year, and Demeter let the grain grow again during that period. The mysteries of Eleusis, celebrated in honor of Demeter and her daughter, seem to have been a ritual enactment of the vegetative cycle suggesting the possibility of human rebirth and resurrection as well. Although the actual rites of this worship are unclear, we know that men as well as women participated in them.

Images of Demeter, therefore, and the famous Homeric hymn in her honor, celebrate both the second and third aspects of mothering, enabling and enduring. In Christian art the third aspect is shown most often in pietàs, which depict Mary receiving her dead son in her arms after he has been taken down from the cross. Although her own suffering is extreme, the mother continues to hold her son, refusing to abandon him in death and disgrace, as most of his followers do. She will also hold together the wavering band of apostles until that first Pentecost in the cenacle when they are at last filled with the strength of the Spirit.

Maternal grieving is memorably presented in the figures of Niobe in Greek myth and Rachel in the Bible. Although not always as dramatic and emotionally powerful as in the reaction to the abduction of Perspehone or the crucifixion of Jesus, sorrow seems always and everywhere to be a part of the mothering function, but it is their endurance that makes Mary and Demeter exemplary. They not only suffer with their children; they hold them throughout their trials. They are emblems of compassion. Bearing the suffering of their children, they go on to integrate its meaning within a life that continues to reach out to others. The mythical Demeter and the human Mary testify to the ability of all individuals to survive chance and death. Demeter points to the renewal of the vegetative cycle as a sign of renewal and rebirth for all living creatures. Mary's endurance of the death of her son without loss of faith or hope testifies to the possibility of human acceptance of death as part of an incomprehensible but ultimately merciful divine process.

In our own century the most poignant artistic rendering of the endurance of mothers is contained in the work of Kathe Kollwitz. After losing her own son in World War I, she led a committed life, working among the poor in Berlin with her doctor-husband. Kollwitz sketched authentic representations of grieving mothers in her etchings, woodcuts and charcoal drawings. These poor women continue to hold their children in the face of harsh social injustice, crying out to the viewer with their pain.

Today newspapers and television place more suffering before our eyes than we can bear: a Vietnamese mother screaming as she runs toward us with her dead baby; Central and South American mothers demanding an account of the "disappeared"; African mothers starving in the desert with their children, looking steadily at us with unbearable patience. Every day we hear of mothers in our cities grieving over children on drugs, in prison, or victimized through gang violence or drunken driving. Of course it is not only mothers who grieve and yet must endure when children suffer, but in life as in art, the terrible pain of losing the life that has been born from your own body seems to be the ultimate human tragedy. We are outraged when we hear of mothers who have gone over the brink, who abuse, even kill their own children. The absence of the mothering we all need at a deep level is as horrifying as its presence is valued.

One other aspect of mothering remains—sharing. I see it in the painting of Isis holding the hand of Queen Nefertiti as they walk, and in the image of Demeter with Persephone after the latter's return from Hades. Homer saw it too, even offered her a kind of exchange:

> you, lady
> who bears
> such great gifts,
> who brings
> the seasons,
> sovereign,
>   Deo,
> you and your
> very beautiful daughter,
>   Persephone,
> be kind, and,
> in exchange for
>   my poem,

give me the kind of life
my heart wants.
        I
will remember you
in my other poems.

Demeter could be said to embody here the virtue of
Erikson's last stage of life, wisdom rather than despair in
the face of death. The need to share is a central human
one, necessary to complete the life cycle. Erik and Joan
Erikson are convinced in their own old age that its wisdom
ties together all the learning born of earlier life crises. It
consists in the ability of the old to be related to younger
generations, not necessarily their own physical descendants, despite their own oncoming death. Most commonly
it is grandparents who achieve this state, but anyone, single or married, who develops a relationship with even one
younger person can be a sharer. The open exchange of
stories between young and old helps both to feel personally related to human community despite the sense of constant change.

There are relatively few examples of the sharing
mother in Christian art, perhaps because there are not
enough in real life, largely because most cultures have not
prepared women for this role. Of those I know, only da
Vinci's painting in the Louvre of St. Ann, Mary and the boy
Jesus together conveys this joyous sense of human sharing
in the Christian story. There may be a suggestion of such a
mother in Quarton's "Coronation of the Virgin," but Mary
is so powerful in that painting that she seems to symbolize
the maternal concern of the divine rather than human
sharing.

The paintings of the Virgin in majesty during the
fourteenth century depict a Mary seated in heaven on a

level with saints, suggesting a kind of comradeship among those who have passed through life's crises. But the equal sharing in these paintings is tempered by the use of gold and the static poses which make it clear that these figures are "in heaven." What is missing is any sense of how humans get there.

Most people today seem uncertain about the existence of heaven, let alone its connection with earth. Living mothers may still be symbols of our most extreme human joy and pain, but they alone cannot connect us with a larger meaning that infuses the unfolding universe and connects us to it. Instead, we are fearful of forces more malevolent than those that nature contains—nuclear destruction, human torture, the decimation of living species, all of them results of human decisions and actions.

I would be distorting the picture of early cultures if I did not add that they had fears of evil forces, and they were well aware of the kind of mothering that could stifle and even annihilate life. Images of the Terrible Mother speak of these negative aspects of mothering and they survive in all cultures—Medusa, Kali, and representations of destructive wombs with sharp teeth. Psychologist Carl Jung theorizes that the many stories of dragon-slaying that occur in the earliest epics of western civilization—for example, in *Beowulf*—represent masculine forces crushing the feminine because of such fears and setting up a civilization based on force and law rather than natural principles.

These mythic triumphs at the dawn of civilization prefigure and partially explain the prevailing male control in all historical societies, which have typically subjugated women and controlled feminine symbols. Appreciation of feminine symbols does not necessarily mean a positive attitude to women. Chinese symbolism could continue to revere the dragon as a sign of immortality even while Chinese customs forced women to bind their feet so that they could neither run nor scarcely imagine a world in which they could live and work as equals. Cultures are often humanly unjust even when their art retains a vision of an earlier, more unified view of life.

Almost the only hint in contemporary art of earlier coherence comes to us from the third world, where men and women have only recently committed the riches of their ancient oral tradition to writing. Not only legends from around the world, but contemporary literature from Africa, for example, is rich in narrative and poetic evocations of the intimate commerce between earth and heaven, all but lost in the experience of colonialism and European missionary teaching. In this literature maternal symbols again represent the support needed throughout this life and as intermediary to the next, as the Mozambican poet Valente Malangatana presents them at the end of his poem "Woman."

> Woman's eye shall open up for me the way to heaven
> Woman's belly shall give birth to me up there
> And woman's glance shall watch me as I go to heaven.

Our contemporary culture insists that airplanes and astronauts rather than angels fly in the skies, and minerals and chemicals rather than ancestors rest in the earth. Even if we reject its either-or assumptions, it is clear that we cannot return to that simple, unified vision of the divine in the natural so prevalent in earlier societies. But neither modern technology nor the mass media have quite destroyed the feeling within us that traditional peoples are ultimately right: the earth *is* our mother. It is sacrilegious to exploit and destroy her. Nor can Americans escape twinges of guilt for what has been done to native Americans who were so willing to share their sacred land with homeless travelers from across the seas.

I do not want to suggest that life in traditional, pagan societies or in medieval Europe was more just, happier, better than in ours. The symbols I have described reflect the human needs and ideals of the cultures that created them, not their historical reality or their social structures. But they do provide evidence that feminine nurturing values were considered essential to human life in those earlier societies.

Nor do I wish to suggest that the visible injustices of our time make it worse than earlier periods. Quite the contrary. The ability of people to learn and deal with each other, aided by technologically advanced means of transportation and communication, makes ours a time of enormous, indeed unique, potential. No good will simply happen, however. It is work to be undertaken because our consciousness is, in fact, torn and divided. The all too rapid and inevitably selective survey I have made of earlier cultures is partly a reflection of my own need—and one I find in many others—to revisit the common human imagination of childhood, seeking resources that may help to overcome fragmentation and separation from others. Our sense of division not only turns us to the past; it prompts us to respond to the present in ways that technology itself makes possible.

Even our divisions, therefore, our sense of being fragmented, can move us to reach out in sympathy to other people around the globe. Perhaps for the first time in history, we are on the verge of developing a human identity and solidarity on a planetary scale. Just as the small child emerges from embeddedness in the maternal environment, so human beings today seem to be on the verge of emergence from embeddedness in limited national and cultural identities.

We are, of course, reminded almost daily that wars are still being fought and blood is being shed in the name of these old identities. But the very awareness of the results of such violence can help give birth to a different consciousness. We can seek to develop a more cooperative kind of relationship better suited to the underlying structure of this planet—a structure biologist Lewis Thomas tells us is like that of a single cell.

The human inhabitants of our world seem to be emerging from a turbulent human adolescence and young adulthood, with its typical exaggeration of sexual differences, its emphasis on aggression and separation. We may at last be on the threshold of an adult, generative period of human development. Just as in the life of an individual, such a development is also a rediscovery of old meaning to be reintegrated into the new identity. More and more people are aware that we are the consciousness of the earth our mother. Now that we are grown up, we must care for her as she continues to care for us. Becoming sharers seems to be our natural destiny.

Such a development will not occur, however, unless we can introduce maternal values into our dominantly patriarchal institutions and public discourse. Earlier I quoted from Brita Stendahl's *Sabbatical Reflections* as she drew on old maternal imagery in her vision of our contemporary needs. But it is good to use other language as well so that people will know I am not simply talking about individual men and women but rather about different attitudes present in every human mind and culture. In terms of spiritual development, such meaning cannot be imposed; it can only be sought.

David Steindl-Rast makes a useful distinction be-

tween purpose and meaning which seems to deal with the
same alternating functions of the human mind for which
others use "feminine" and "masculine." With purposes,
he says, we must be active and take control: "The whole of
modern life tends to be thus purpose-oriented." But
meaning is different; it consists of savoring, not using, the
world around us. "Our goal is to let meaning flow into our
purposeful activities by fusing activity and passivity into
genuine responsiveness." First, however, we must feel the
need to let it flow and transform us.

For those like myself, raised in a church that lives in
creative tension with the Bible, it might seem that we are
today being given another chance at the task assigned to
human beings in the book of Genesis. This time, however,
each of us is asked to give conscious attention and to make
an active contribution to nurturing and naming that part of
the world that lies within our power. Can we live in peace
and justice with the real people who inhabit this earth, as
John XXIII's vision asks? For a long time the projects for
world development have been carried out by political and
economic forces that saw no role for religion. Yet today we
should be able to see that the need to work cooperatively
with people around the globe fuses the religious and the
human obligation; the two are intimately connected.

Earlier cultures united the human search for meaning
in their lives through maternal symbols. But how can religions mediate such meaning today when they and their
symbols are still fighting "holy" wars against each other,
thinking of themselves as the sole mediators of meaning?
Or when they are split internally, unable to see the need
for common growth rather than the imposition of ideas
and identity from one side to the other?

I make no claims to a grand theory; I have no all-
encompassing vision of inevitable growth. But my experi-

ence as a mother and teacher makes me see parallels between what individuals must do and what the human race
needs to do. Steindl-Rast's distinction between purpose
and meaning helps me to describe that task. The eighteen
year olds in my class have a purpose; they want to become
successful, "winners." Of course, as they learn more
about the world and other people, they will find out how
realistic or even desirable such purposes really are. What
faith should add to their search is the emphasis on self-
respect and the sacredness of all persons, forcing them to
recognize the tension between social pressures to exploit
and their inner desire to share. Human beings as a whole
are in the same situation; the main difference between
them is that some have far more control over the earth's
resources than others.

The maternal symbols of other cultures revisited in
this chapter remind us that we need to be held in order to
hold. Those who have made the difficult journey to integration may be strengthened and enlightened by the support of others, as Madonna Kolbenschlag was, to move
toward a coherent world vision:

> I have learned in the company of whole and holy
> women to exorcise the unreal, to celebrate and
> ritualize the true and the real, to speak and hear a
> new language, to feel the spirit through flesh and
> matter, to see everything *from within,* as if cre-
> ation were the Womb of God where, although we
> experience darkness and obscurity, there is also
> warmth, nourishment, movement, growth, con-
> nection and delight.

Where are the rest of us to turn for the holding that
can help us break through to such understanding? Where

can we find the life-preserving power to reverse the destructive thrust of our own culture, in which the absence of mothering is palpable in the daily abuse of people and nature? Traditional maternal symbols reveal that beneficient mothering has traditionally been a male and continuingly divine activity as well as a female one. If we all need to be held today, we may have to rediscover that the four aspects of mothering—protecting, enabling, enduring and sharing—lie within ourselves and the small communities to which we relate.

Striving to integrate our faith into our lives, actions and decisions, we will be nurturing ourselves and learning to let go, enduring when we must and starting to share where we may not have been able to before. Looking freshly at the human sources of our faith, inspired by Spirit, we will be incorporating the attitudes and functions of mothering into our work and ourselves.

5

Real Mothers:
Vulnerable Sharers

Sometimes when I see a young mother with a baby I feel the same sudden joy that I receive when standing in front of a great artist's rendering of the nativity. On other occasions, passing by a woman whose drawn face tells me that her child is in trouble, there is a stab of anguished sympathy like that I feel in front of a pietà. Despite the clichés of commercial exploitation, mothers still seem to embody the most intense joy and the deepest pain possible to the human condition. No wonder artists have chosen them as subjects throughout the ages: mothers are natural icons.

But I have no intention of repeating what has been done to mothers for centuries—of interpreting them in terms of my feelings, more detached now that my own mother is long dead and all my children live elsewhere. No group has ever been more defined, analyzed, or advised on their nature and responsibilities than mothers—almost always by men acting out of their own needs or hopes, or their interpretation of society's good. And in the past mothers have usually tried to fit in, to live up to the expectations of others.

As they face up to all the demands placed upon them

today, however, they are also telling us that we have been mistaken about those expectations. They know better than any others that they cannot raise even their own children by themselves in a society which does not take their own experience seriously. For the first time many are calling attention in public to their own inadequacy, acknowledging their vulnerability in the face of social, economic and interpersonal conditions they cannot control. In their struggle to become fully contributing members to the wider society, contemporary mothers are reminding us that we are all vulnerable and interdependent, no matter how much the individualism and separations of our culture blind us to this reality.

When we see a mother gripping a toddler with one hand and carrying a bag of groceries with the other, we are visibly reminded that some people care for others, share and suffer with others who are learning to negotiate their next stage of development. But if we try to grasp that mother's experience from her point of view, we will no longer see her just as a symbol or a "natural" protector of the young and helpless, whom society should revere as long as she devotes herself exclusively to that task. It is only realistic to recognize that she is quite capable of yelling at the little boy a few minutes later or slapping him as he reaches for a candy bar. The most instructive approach is to regard her first as a human being who can help us learn what produces the kind of relationship that satisfies her, her children and our sensibilities.

After observing them closely and dispassionately, I can say that mothers almost always want to be good mothers. But if they try to fit into a role or live up to an ideal, they will find it almost impossible. When their lack of attention to self-knowledge and development is reinforced by social pressure, they will no longer trust their own instincts or make the best use of their abilities. They and their families will suffer. Such a cramped exercise of motherhood has a long and painful history. Observations from life and literature have helped me see why contemporary women can no longer carry out other people's assumptions, and why the new consciousness mothers are forging is so significant and hopeful for the rest of us.

Charles Dickens provides perhaps the most extreme example of the effect of the social control of mothers in the figure of Mrs. Gradgrind in *Hard Times.* The perfect wife to Thomas Gradgrind, educator, philanthropist, and eventually Member of Parliament, who submits his family to his well-intentioned theories, she is so lacking in self that she cannot raise her children. The responsibility of mothering gives her a headache, but she doesn't even know that the pain is hers. As she tries to carry out the overly rational educational schemes of her husband, she never sees that she has a role in developing her children's imagination or conscience, since her own have long been stifled. The result is that she leaves the children helpless before the self-deceivers who exploit them and the country's economy. Dickens make it plain that the Victorian fathers who gave lip-service to the ideal of motherhood were trying to control mothering for their own purposes, and in the process destroyed children, families and their own humanity.

Paternal control has not always been so clearly malignant for individuals as it was in nineteenth century England, but for centuries, in very different cultures, it has consistently been exercised without a thought of consulting women. Social anthropologist Sheila Kilzinger provides a telling example when she reports that one of the most brilliant studies of an earlier culture—Evans Pritchard's studies of the Nuer of the Sudan (1940)—mentions women less often than cows. This may reflect accurately the way Nuer men saw their culture, she tells us, but it leaves us uninformed about how fifty percent of the Nuer tribe understood their lives. Although our culture talks far more about women, it has been almost equally blind to the subjective strengths of mothers.

As mothers experience it, the cultural definition of their role, and even its idealization, have been the other face of neglect. What was true of the Nuer tribe has also been true of Kikuyu, Chinese, and pre-World War II Americans: all women were presumed to be potential mothers, which was their highest (and often, only) calling, and were therefore to be controlled by confinement to private life. Paradoxically, as technological progress and social welfare increased, actual mothers were in fact given less public support. Women were still seen primarily as sex objects and homemakers, pressed into early marriage and motherhood. I have learned about the subjective effects of such contemporary control from thirty-five and forty-five year old women students trying to recover from the disasters of their early marriages.

Given little or no preparation for raising children, these women usually became exclusively responsible for this task. Adrift both psychologically and economically, they were expected not only to devote themselves completely to bringing up their children, but to find happiness in doing so. Political scientist Mary O'Brien, a native of Scotland now teaching in Canada, insists that women's support for other women in pregnancy and childbirth, which she observed repeatedly in the poorest sections of Glasgow, is almost completely absent in North America. Repeated media emphasis on the stories of glamorous women executives may prompt many to forget that careers for married women have in fact not been available until quite recently. Even in the 1950s friends of mine were immediately fired from their jobs—or left under the pressure of convention—as soon as they were married. Even today married women with children face far more restricted job and career choices than men, though most will have to work to pay the family bills.

Since society still considers mothers to be primarily responsible for the young, if children are abused, on drugs, or in prison, mothers who work or are on welfare are the first to be blamed. As news reports constantly increase our awareness of the breakdown of our system of child-raising, many put the blame squarely on women for abandoning their "traditional place." The dominant cultural attitude to mothers is deeply ambivalent, ready to enshrine unreal models who "existed only for their children," and quick to blame real mothers when young people do not live up to its hopes.

Clearly, it is no solution to transfer the blame to men or to present all mothers as heroines. In cases of failure there is almost always a cultural collaboration. For example, although we are rightly shocked when we hear of the many men who have abused their children, studies show that such men have themselves frequently been abused when they were young. Women who collaborate in such abuse, or are too weak to take realistic steps to help prevent it, have usually been similar victims when they were girls. If we are all responsible for the world's children, we will have to consult mothers who know the cost before we unthinkingly invoke tradition or presume to establish new guidelines for how children are to be brought up. When we talk about "restoring family values" without such a thoughtful examination, it may be merely code language for preserving an unjust and unworkable system at the expense of women, of course, but ultimately of all of us.

All too often such old assumptions linger on unchallenged even in the minds of intelligent and generous men. Last summer, for example, my husband and I rented a cottage for a few weeks next door to a kindly retired doctor, still mourning the death of his wife, a working and living partner for some fifty years. Over a drink one night he offered his considered explanation for the ills of today's society: "Feminization." I am afraid his judgment is shared by many other good men who are quick to blame social and economic dislocation on mothers who don't "stay home." No one has helped them recognize the deleterious effects of such attitudes on those mothers who can afford to make that choice, or the economic reality which determines that even those who might prefer to work in the house are usually forced to help support their families by working at unrewarding jobs with inadequate child-care services.

Above all, we need genuine public debate in which mothers are equal participants. Present assumptions about their responsibility for bringing up children, even when it is less doctrinaire than the doctor's, simply does not confront reality. It does, however, accurately reflect a culture which basically has tried to sentimentalize and get away from mothers without taking the trouble to understand them as human beings.

Ironically, often tragically, society sends contradictory signals to mothers, leaving them deeply divided about their role. Such ambivalence has produced a masochistic parody of selflessness in many mothers, not just in the extreme case of a Mrs. Gradgrind, but even among contemporary, well-educated women. Friends of mine in their seventies tell me that they are only now seeing clearly and regretting their own earlier tendencies to please, to defer, and to conform, even though at the time they thought they were independent.

I first encountered this complex combination of attitudes in my own mother. Many times she told me how grateful she had been for my arrival; I was her first child. She had prayed for a child to St. Ann, mother of Mary, and when I arrived, she made a pilgrimage of thanks to the shrine of St. Ann de Beaupre in Quebec. Sadly, I now recognize that my being wanted grew, however unintentionally, out of her need to establish herself as full wife to my father, a widower with two children. The resulting family dynamics were played out at some cost to my older brother and sister, though as a child I enjoyed being so loved by a mother who was both charming and talented. Even so, I could never understand the value she placed on motherhood. It was a slow walk with my mother if we met a woman on the sidewalk pushing a baby carriage. My mother would immediately smile at an absolute stranger, coo at her baby, and to my intense boredom engage the other mother in lively conversation about feeding, clothing, and exercise.

"Motherhood is the highest calling anyone can have," she would tell me, looking dreamy. I retained a certain skepticism because I saw there was another side to the story. I not only had an uneasy sense that her love was not being equally shared among us children, but was also aware of my mother's several miscarriages and her generally frail health. Much later, when I told her I was going to be married, she instinctively exclaimed, "Oh, you're too young to have to get into that constant subjection to doctors!" Until I became a mother myself, I could not understand either her passionate love of babies, her sense of physical vulnerability, or her inability to treat her children with equal fairness.

At that crucial time in my own development, when I needed to find new meaning in my spiritual life to strengthen my adult self, the church's standard preaching that all women were "by nature" spiritual mothers simply increased a sense of inadequacy which I have found to be almost endemic among mothers. Motherhood was lavishly praised, of course, especially on Christmas and Mother's Day. But the other side of such idealization was that, with the exception of John XXIII, popes in my lifetime have continued to envision women's total lives and careers in terms of two possible alternatives: motherhood or virginity. They seemed unaware of the male bias or the injustice involved in defining women exclusively by their relation to sex and others, oblivious to the psychological and spiritual stifling such definitions imposed on their human development.

I think particularly of several close friends who could not have children or could have only one, and who could never be convinced—even by loving, supportive husbands—that their lives were not largely wasted. They acted as if their talents and human potential were unimportant, and in the process sometimes closed off opportunities to make full use of their intelligence and skills, as if physical motherhood was the only way of doing God's will. Sadness and inner discontent were the inevitable results of this misguided self-constriction, largely due to their internalization of ecclesiastical and social norms. The results injured countless husbands and children as well.

Shortly after my first child was born, I heard a Mother's Day sermon that appalled me. A young curate told us about the death of his mother at the age of fifty-three. He had felt a pang of sorrow and loss, he told us, but then he realized that all her children had found their niche in life, so that her role as a mother was complete. He could now rejoice at her return "home."

It was my reaction to such homilies, as well as to the

ordinary teaching of popes and pastors on women's role in church and society, that impelled me to do research among other women as a form of networking for survival. The official language I was hearing employed a static terminology that seemed largely irrelevant to the constantly changing demands of life.

Whatever the reasons why pastors and many religion teachers tell women that it is their "nature" or their "role" to be mothers—good intentions, false idealism, self-deluding projections, or simple ignorance—they are defeating the very purposes they hope to achieve. Women who believe that they are by nature able to mother will not develop the interpersonal skills they need, and those who believe they have to fit into an externally determined role will not feel free to function as the fully responsive human beings that are needed for this demanding task.

Controls, ideals and definitions from outside don't help because the reality of motherhood is always unexpected. What a first-time mother most needs is confidence-building experiences in dealing with others. No simple preparation exists to turn a young woman quickly into someone responsible for herself and another completely dependent human being, and all too little attention has been given to thinking about what would help her. In addition, the arrival of a child occurs within a wide variety of family contexts, each of which produce multiple and often conflicting demands. It is unrealistic to expect that today's young women, who are increasingly apt to have grown up in small families with little experience in dealing with children, will know how to love and raise children simply by feminine instinct and find their chief happiness in doing so. A young mother often finds herself at the center of a cyclone of expectations and demands no one has told her about, much less coached her to deal with, but she is still expected to behave like a seasoned athlete, an economist, a philosopher-psychologist, even a saint.

The first time I found this reality expressed accurately from the mother's viewpoint was in Tillie Olsen's *Silences:*

> More than in any other human relationship, over-whelmingly more, motherhood means being instantly interruptable, responsive, responsible. Children need one *now* (and remember, in our society, the family must often try to be the center for love and health the outside world is not). The very fact that these are real needs, that one feels them as one's own (love, not duty), *that there is no one else responsible for these needs,* gives them primacy. It is distraction, not meditation, that becomes habitual; interruption, not continuity; spasmodic, not constant toil.

Turning eagerly to Olsen's fiction, I discovered that the mothers in her stories were strong models of endurance, pilgrims on the road to sharing. Anna in *Yonnondio From the Thirties* and Eva in *Tell Me a Riddle* reveal the immemorial struggles of mothers striving to help their children against great odds, fighting a world of economic and social limitations they cannot control. The theme is struck by the mother in "I Stand Here Ironing," the first of her stories Olsen thought worthy of publication:

> She was a beautiful baby. She blew shining bubbles of sound. She loved motion, loved light, loved color and music and textures. She would lie on the floor in her blue overalls patting the surface so hard in ecstasy her hands and feet would blur. She was a miracle to me, but when she was

> eight months old I had to leave her daytimes with
> the woman downstairs to whom she was no mira-
> cle at all, for I worked or looked for work and for
> Emily's father, who "could no longer endure"
> (he wrote in his good-bye note) "sharing want
> with us."

Still thinking of her daughter, she realizes "all that is in
her will not bloom." But she accepts life's limitations,
hoping only that "There is still enough to live by . . . that
she is more than this dress on the ironing board, helpless
before the iron."

Olsen's *Yonnondio* has a special power because it
shows how even a loving family can be destroyed when
babies keep coming in families without the means to support them. Anna and Jim are poor, hard-working parents
struggling to make a better life for their children. Everywhere they turn, they are prevented from fulfilling this
simple ambition. Ground down by economic want, unjust
working conditions and Anna's continued pregnancies,
the fragile web of love and joy is torn apart, and they begin
to hurt each other.

Because they cannot cope with teachers or social
workers as equals, Anna and Jim are unable to defend the
sensitive, intelligent children these authority figures see
as ignorant farm kids. "Yonnondio," an Indian word Olsen
found in a Whitman poem, is a lament for those who have
died leaving no voice to record their passage. Olsen's
novel is her lament for the fate of loving parents—particularly mothers—unable to make the choices needed to fulfill their hopes for their family.

Olsen's mother at the ironing board wants her daughter to have choices; the heroine of Margaret Atwood's
classic novel of feminine self-discovery, *Surfacing*, echoes

this aspiration: "This above all, to refuse to be a victim." The heroine returns with friends to the scene of her childhood in a remote lake region of Quebec in search of her missing father—and for meaning that might motivate her to go on living. Searching for primitive Indian signs deep beneath the lake which might have attracted her father, she encounters the need to seek the primitive in herself. She sends her friends away, fasts, and carries out her own psychic healing. When she can at last see the spirits of her parents, she can also forgive herself for the early abortion she underwent for the convenience of her older, married lover. Now that she is able to accept her past, she can begin to think of a possible future. She chooses to bear a child.

The ability to make a decision that she can live with (and not necessarily before she conceives) is essential to a woman's ability to become fully human. I was convinced of the importance of women's ability to choose whether or not to marry or to have children through my own experience, reading and the personal stories other women shared with me in 1965. One mother wrote then:

> The sixth baby finished me. It took me so long to learn—twelve years—that I had to make my *own* decisions. Many of the serious emotional problems in our marriage were not necessary. How I wish that I had been taught there were no simple answers, only the complex standards of generosity, and the personal freedom necessary to live up to it.

This kind of freedom is neither selfish in a superficial sense, nor idealistic in an unreal sense. It is a slow creation involving the self-discipline necessary to make more sensi-

ble responses to a unique and complex set of circumstances. Even to be conscious of conflicts and limitations is
an awakening for a woman, a step on the way to learning
that life is not a matter of following external guides,
whether they are idealized, or come from cultural and economic pressures. I am saddened to see how many young
women still do not really seem free to plan a life, even
partially. They are so caught up in the whirl of pressures to
buy, conform, and please (or succeed) in which sexual relations are now so expected, that it is only after they become pregnant that they begin to see the need to make
decisions and abide by them. Though it is much harder
then and their choices more limited, many then move
beyond role-playing to deal with their real situation. They
know better than any others how much better mothers
they might have been if they had had the strength and
freedom to do that earlier.

Mothering is, above all, an art, something that can't
be done by rote. Each child is unique; even bathing and
feeding a baby is impossible unless done spontaneously,
not mechanically. Almost every action involved in rearing
a child requires instant decision-making by a confident parent. Moreover, the extreme intimacy of the mother-child
relationship means that powerful negative feelings will
emerge and must be acknowledged and dealt with. The
mother who thinks her role is always to be "good" will
find it very difficult to acknowledge her anger and frustration because she "isn't supposed" to have such feelings.
She will waste her time repressing her feelings—which
are important signs to which she should pay attention—
instead of learning how to deal with the situations that
cause them.

I learned a great deal about this process from the students who shared their experiences in mothering classes.

It took a long time, for example, for Virginia to admit that she often lost her temper with her children. She looked guilty when she finally confessed to this weakness: "Mothers are supposed to be serene." But blaming herself prevented her from thinking about the cause of her anger. She thought she was a bad mother because she yelled at her children; then she would try to make it up to them, she told us, by baking brownies. In fact, she was confusing them: maybe it was smart to get mommy angry!

Listening to other parents in the class, Virginia came to realize that it was perfectly natural, almost inevitable, to get angry at children sometimes. Extreme love is always accompanied by the possibility of its opposite when something in the relationship is disappointing. Gradually she came to see her anger as an opportunity: first, to acknowledge her own feelings, and, second, to begin to probe her motivation so as to deal with it constructively. Next she learned how to share her feelings with her children so that they could understand them, too. "I'm very angry at you for breaking the heads off the three kings. I brought those figures all the way from France so that we could put them under the tree every Christmas."

This kind of communication, the kind Chaim Genott advocated in his popular books on parenting, neither demeans nor confuses children but helps them see the situation accurately and gives them a chance to respond positively. "We can glue them together." "I can paint the cracks." Learning to use it helped Virginia become a better nurturing mother (the first task) and gave her the self-confidence that set her on the way to becoming an effective enabler (the second).

Some mothers are exceptionally successful in raising their children to deal with reality even though they live in seemingly impossible circumstances. Over the years I have heard from a number of my black students about mothers who seemed so powerful to them as children that they feared them more than any street toughs or drug pushers. The stories they told help me believe in the determined mother Richard Wright describes in "The Street," who sends her young son back to the store over and over again, despite the beatings he receives from bullies on the block, until he learns how to survive. Telling the story from the son's point of view, however, the author does not reveal the cost of such a policy to the mother.

More protected mothers have different problems; internalizing motherhood as a total role is one. It blinds them to other possibilities and hurts their ability to mother well. When we asked mothers in the course to share their birthing experiences, Florence rhapsodized about the joy of her only son's arrival. Only much later, when other mothers had begun to talk openly about painful aspects of their relations with adolescent children, Florence reluctantly admitted that she had lately been upset because her relations with her son were no longer harmonious. Jim was criticizing her for the very things he seemed to love earlier; sometimes he even made her cry. When a bit of questioning revealed that Jim was now fifteen, the class almost as one assured Florence that it was high time he criticized her; she should have anticipated it. "Don't take it personally," they counseled her. That will only make it more difficult for Jim to make the necessary transition to psychological independence. If he can't do that, he can never move from embeddedness in her life and values to his own identity, from which he can then relate to her again as a loving adult.

The other women in class gave Florence just the shove she needed to move from her all-inclusive self-conception as a protecting mother to a tentative new identity as an enabling mother—and to let go. She had found it unthinkable before, because, like the priest who gave that awful Mother's Day sermon, she had totally absorbed the idea that there could be nothing for her after motherhood.

In our technologically advanced world, of course, the reality is that raising children takes less time out of a much longer life than it used to. And being able to envision a future for herself after the early intimate years of motherhood is an essential part of a mother's ability to help children grow up. In our first class a disillusioned grandmother shared her disappointment about motherhood; she had expected to be honored in her old age. Instead, her children were busy with their own lives; they had almost no contact with her. "I was brought up to expect that my children would be my happiness," she complained bitterly, using almost the same words as the Nigerian mother in Buchi Emecheta's ironic novel *The Joys of Motherhood*, which reveals the universality of the sentiment. To some extent, the older cultures (whether African tribal or earlier American) supported women in traditional roles and made it less necessary for them to have independence of thought and action. That is not the case today, when we can also see more clearly the injustice that accompanied the suppression of women in those earlier cultures. As for ours, Adrienne Rich accurately observes, "It is not enough to let children go; we need selves of our own to return to." Rich insists that the conflicts and difficulties of mothers and children are related, and so is their development; one cannot thrive at the cost of the other. Recent research on mothers by Willard confirms her view:

> Mothering, which brings with it the necessity to make choices that involve the well-being of oneself and others, provides an opportunity to rede-

fine one's understanding of the place of the self in
such decisions.

An important part of the growing ability to make such
choices is a mother's skillfulness in communicating. Sometimes it is hard to develop a voice that a husband can hear.
The age-old difficulty men have in hearing what women
have to say finds striking expression in Mary Wilkins Free-
man's late nineteenth century short story "The Revolt of
Mother." The husband in this story, Adoniram Penn,
seems constitutionally unable to hear his patient, hard-
working wife when she reminds him how much she and
the children need the house he promised to build her ever
since they were married. Over and over she pleads until
he simply walks out. Penn is secretly putting up yet another ample barn for his cattle. Although Sarah appeals to
him with every reasonable, moral argument at her com-
mand, he never responds.

When providence sends him away to buy a horse,
Sarah Penn determinedly moves into the new barn with
the children. To the village's amazement, and despite the
admonitions of the minister, she refuses to leave. When
Adoniram comes home and finds his family in the barn, he
eats his favorite meal in stunned silence, then goes out to
sit dumbly on the front steps. At the end, accepting the *fait
accompli*, he says to his wife, "Why, Sarah, why didn't you
tell me it meant so much to you?"

One of my more recent students is a modern-day
Sarah Penn; what Marie needed was not a house but a way
to connect the private, wife-and-mother-person she had
become—a champion baker for Lutheran church sales—
with her need to think and relate to others as a social being. Little wonder that she was depressed; psychologist
Robert Kegan interprets depression precisely as "not

knowing" how I and the world cohere. The increasing number of depressed mothers represent women who have given up the struggle to make sense out of their lives; they also often produce negative and sometimes violent outcomes for their children.

Marie, on the other hand, was determined to find out how she and the world cohered. Over her husband's objections, which at times turned into threats of violence, she took some college courses. She knew that he felt he was somehow failing to satisfy her as he should. When a fellow student handed her Carol Gilligan's article on "Woman's Place in Man's Life Cycle," she felt confirmed in her determination to keep up her studies and convince her husband no matter what it took. She was certain that learning would only strengthen the marriage to which she was fully committed. It took about two years and the support of his parents for Marie to turn him around with her steadfastness as Sarah did Adoniram. She now serves on the adult student advisory board and both children and husband are proud of her.

General wisdom still contends that emphasis on the self is selfish. Social psychologist Erich Fromm, however, insists that selfishness is not identical with self-love but with its very opposite. Current research suggests that as women develop a stronger sense of self, they move toward interdependence, or the kind of mutual loving that Fromm depicts as fully human.

I realized in the late 1970s that this ability to be connected with others without losing one's self was just what I, as a child, feared was not possible for women. I had observed the mysterious phenomenon of lively young women who married and had children and suddenly seemed to disappear. Looking back, I realized that for a time in my marriage I too had been swallowed up inside my house, and the effects were as sinister as my childish fears had painted them. I began merely *reacting* to the powerful institutions that touched my family. I often adopted a defensive stance to schoolteachers and administrators, one they may have been responsible for encouraging but which was not in the best interest of the children we wanted to educate.

When I timorously took a small step "outside" into the community by teaching a course at the local college, I found that the double perspective gave me a better sense of what problems were real and some of the self-confidence needed to cope with them. I began to realize that those grammar school teachers who had intimidated me when they explained that my oldest son was an underachiever had their own insecurities; representatives of authority with which everyone has to deal in the normal course of events, from the town clerk to the policeman on the highway, were caught up in their own bureaucratic systems and were largely powerless to change them. I no longer had unrealistic fears of them nor was under the illusion that they could solve any significant problems. I was learning to dig beneath my fears and their instinctive submission to a rule in order to work together to find some common ground.

I began to understand my mother better; she had felt the double bind implied in her intense desire to be a good mother and the contrary signals that such a role didn't count for much in the "real" world. Because she wasn't able to find a way to be herself in ever-widening circles from the home, she lived too much through her children. Despite the disintegration and chaos of today's social environment, it is easier than in her generation for women to become interdependent, to remain the same people while moving through their multiple roles and relationships, private and public, and this helps them as well as everyone they deal with.

When mothers can reach this kind of self-acceptance, the ambivalence they often feel about their role becomes transformed into an ability to tolerate difference and ambiguity in others, even their own children. Thinking more clearly, using their imaginations more creatively, they can recognize and respond to the broken relationships and stilted conversations that cry out to their ability to mend.

In class we regularly heard about failures in communication between parents, older children and in-laws. Mothers confessed their fear of Thanksgiving dinners filled with false, formal talk, or of flowers received on Mother's Day despite strained and often unexpressed feelings. Too often they continue to blame themselves; even when they manage to avoid feeling guilt, they keep thinking of what else they might have done—something more, something better. Like the mother at the ironing board in Olsen's story, they know that they may have demanded more of older children than they should. Like her, too, when they want to talk to their grown children, they often have to face the fact that these new adults are preoccupied with their own affairs and shrink their parents to one-dimensional memories.

It is a common theme in recent women's fiction. Think of the narrator of Alice Walker's *The Color Purple,* a vulnerable girl who becomes a loving force able to care for those who have not cared for her. Walker's search through memory for the source of her mother's and grandmother's power in poverty and slavery reveals the source of her own inner strength and creativity. It also brings to public awareness the subjective reality of African-American experience we could never otherwise have shared. Probing the subjective reality of black mothers long dead who refused to be simply victims, the novels of Toni Morrison, too, particularly *Beloved*, are another important resource for cultural healing across our racial barriers.

Mothers, and even grandmothers, who finally achieve the self-direction to pursue goals they choose to follow, can be mediators of connectedness across dividing-lines of sex as well as generation and culture. This feminine path is powerfully conveyed by Eva, the grandmother in Tillie Olsen's *Tell Me a Riddle*, who has been forced to live according to "the rhythms of others." When all her children are grown and gone, her husband is willing to accept a comic role as senior citizen in the Happy Haven retirement home, but she is not. She fights fiercely for the self no one ever gave her time or encouragement to shape before; she studies and reflects, rejecting the grandmotherly role her children assume she will love. They do not really know her, but even as she is dying of cancer, she is able to recall and reaffirm the idealism of her revolutionary youth in Russia. And in her deathbed ravings, she is at last able to summon her husband to join her in lamenting the loss of their old dreams, the human solidarity they had shared, which he had been ready to trade for superficial comfort and company. As Eva suffers and dies, she passes on the meaning she has discovered, the coherence she needs, to her grieving husband, who had almost forgotten he needs it too.

Though some men are as hard of hearing as Eva's husband, sooner or later many come to realize that they too are both vulnerable and interdependent. Mothers have no innate moral superiority; they are merely obvious symbols of a reality we all share. Habits of individualism, ideals of an overly abstract freedom, provide partially distorting lenses through which we view the world, but they do not describe what we actually experience. Our actual interdependence is so obvious that we frequently fail to notice it.

A summary of a typical morning's activities offers familiar examples of what I mean. I visited the doctor, and he told the nurse to give me an injection. I had to trust that the nurse, the doctor, the people who made and packed the needle which penetrated my skin, were all honest and competent, doing their job properly. When I asked the nurse how they handled waste disposal, she said that they send it away on trucks that are privately owned but don't follow them to the dumping site. We have to trust again—that it won't end up on a beach. Everytime we get on a plane, we are dependent on the pilot and the mechanics; if we should be especially unlucky, we will even be dependent on the desperate calculations of terrorists. And so it goes with almost everything we do, almost everything we eat. We live by faith.

All too often it is not justified; we need vigilant consumer groups to check on political collusion, health hazards, product safety. And every so often events occur that reveal how vulnerable we all are in the face of chance and death. Less than a week ago a colleague of mine was killed instantaneously in an auto accident by a driver whose truck had not passed inspection and whose brakes failed. She was only thirty-seven years old and eight months pregnant with her first natural child, who was also killed. Her distraught husband was left with the two young children they had already adopted, for she was as dedicated to mothering in life as she was to writing about it in literature. If only the driver had thought about how his reckless independence would affect others! Precisely because they realize so well that they can never completely control their lives or protect the lives of those they love, mothers remind us to be more conscious of the reality of interdependence, especially of the vulnerability of others to our decisions.

Some contemporary men, when their eyes and ears are sensitive, are also able to turn the vulnerability they come to recognize unexpectedly into clarified vision and declarations of interdependence. The distinguished American Protestant theologian Reinhold Niebuhr passed through such an experience late in his life. An energetic man whose insights on the ethical implications of public policy gained serious public consideration from national leaders as well as political philosophers, Niebuhr's life was dramatically changed in 1952 by a series of neurological attacks that left him weakened and partly paralyzed. This personal tragedy, however, led him to new vision, as he told Larry Rasmussen:

> The physical ills that consigned me to the "sidelines" were productive in furnishing me with insights about human nature that had never occurred to me before. I learned to know the goodness of men and women who went out of their way to help an invalid. Among the persons who impressed me with their helpfulness were my doctors, nurses, and therapists, my colleagues and friends in the realms of both politics and religion. I soon learned that some of these people showed an almost charismatic gift of love.

The experience made him change some of his earlier judgments, particularly when it came to the editing and revising of his work done by his wife, to whom he had until this time ascribed goodness as part of her nature as a woman. Again, as he told Rasmussen:

I had never measured the depth and breadth of her devotion until I was stricken. It may be an indication of my male pride that I had only casually relied on her superior sense of style in editing my books and articles. Now I absolutely relied on her editing, and it dealt not only with style but, more and more, with the substance of her thought.

Again and again she assured me that I would do as much for her, were she ill. But I doubted it, because I was inclined to affirm the superior *agape* of a woman.

In his vulnerable, interdependent old age, Niebuhr could more than ever affirm the wisdom of the prayer he had composed earlier, which so well combined feminine and masculine insights into a unified, human petition: "God, give us grace to accept with serenity the things that cannot be changed, courage to change the things that should be changed, and the wisdom to distinguish the one from the other."

An experience of vulnerability also deepened and integrated the spiritual identity of Thomas Merton, one of the most profound and widely read spiritual writers of our time. While recovering from surgery at the age of fifty-two, he fell in love with his nurse. The poems he wrote to "M" reveal the powerful liberating aspect of this experience for Merton. Struggling to find meaning in his monastic life, he had begun to feel fractured in himself, to lose the overall meaning parts of his faith had had for him. He had clung so hard to a perfectionist spirituality that it had nearly shattered him.

Now he discovered that healing could come through the heat and light kindled by sharing in the woundedness of another. His tendency to separate human and divine love gave way through need to an acceptance of his humanity as part of God's will:

> If we fail or refuse
> To lay bare
> Our own essential anguish
> If we do not by ourselves
> Invent our own remedy . . .
> The newest love in the world
> (That ancient and first love that was new
> In the unheard of beginning)
> The world will not begin again
> Tomorrow
> It will cease to exist.

When mothers gain self-confidence, bolstered by their integration into the wider community, those who are also believers can help us see that self-discovery, in a context of interdependence, is also a rediscovery of the human face of the church. They show us how to continue this rediscovery through a similar process of growth. Joan Bel Geddes' account of how charity begins with oneself, of how she grew to become a strong, caring person has a prophetic dimension, because it clarifies the spiritual and theological imperatives that are bound up in the process. Already a writer and a specialist in child care, Bel Geddes described her inner transformation from perfectionist to fallible human being as a spiritual advance. A convert to Catholicism and a wife and mother, she tried to follow the available spiritual advice with its emphasis on asceticism, its call to a life of perfection. She found it impossible; like Virginia, the woman in my course, she would unaccountably lose her temper while trying to "live up" to her ideals. Spiritual discipline, a direct attempt to overcome her faults, made not a jot of difference in her ability to lead a daily life of homely charity.

After her husband divorced her, and an initial period of self-hatred and extreme vulnerability, with the help of group therapy she began to change. She grew to see herself as the group saw her and liked her, as the funny, intelligent woman she actually was. It is odd, she comments, that the Bible tells us to love others as we love ourselves, while religious teachers so often leave out one-third of that equation, that we should love ourselves. Everyday reality should make us realize that we cannot love others unless we have a self to love them with.

Margaret Hebblethwaite presents an unsentimental insider's look at what it takes to mother young children in her *Mothering and God.* With a mind trained in philosophy and theology she analyzes the pressures of family life, and discovers that the strong emotions aroused by motherhood and the "everyday slog of bringing up children" find their true meaning as part of a relationship with God. She is unusually honest about what it is like to be the mother of a two year old who constantly attacks his baby sister. What makes it so unbelievably exhausting is that "a mother cannot escape when the situation becomes intolerable." Hebblethwaite insists on the same need for a breathing space, a time of peace to collect and calm herself, and reveals the same sense of failure that was expressed again and again in mothering classes.

Husbands and friendly adults simply do not comprehend the strain experienced by such a mother; however well-intentioned, they are only maddening when they counsel patience. Hebblethwaite's diary of a single day spent entirely with very young children helps us see why this healthy, caring, stay-at-home mother once ran screaming into the street to reduce the tension.

When she is able to admit her need for help and gets it—someone to help out a few days a week so that she can study at the Gregorian University in Rome where her husband is then working—she is able to restore herself and finds she has become a better mother. Where she had been mistaken, she tells us, was in "sacrificing herself," for her children. A mother tries to give her children all the support she can, but if she neglects herself, she hurts them as much as herself. She needs time "to pick up the pieces, time to stoke her fires of imagination," so that when she sees her child running up to her "she may respond with unfeigned pleasure."

The time spent away from her children brings an enlarged perspective which enables her to become a true vulnerable sharer, eager to tell us what mothering has revealed to her about God's action in our lives:

> There is a mother who lives up to our hopes, though we are not she. There is a love that cannot be damaged, though we do not possess it. We have already drunk deeply, more deeply than we knew, of that divine love, and have let our children drink of it through us. But it is not ours to give forever, it does not originate in us. We must turn back, and drink again, like children, trust again, pray again, depend again. Then, strengthened and consoled by our mother, we can be a mother again to our little ones, letting maternity flow through us, not from us but from God.

Because mothers are so deeply aware of their own inadequacy, they quite naturally remind us that God alone is the perfect mother, and in so doing summon up the significant but long-neglected tradition in the church which gives expression to the feminine aspects of God. Such reminders should also prompt us to uncover, perhaps for the first time, the human dimension of the mother of Jesus, to think of what it cost her to make the decisions she did, without the support or understanding of the legal or religious officials of her time. It is to Mary's humanity that we must look today if we are to understand and imitate this woman who has always been honored in Catholic tradition as the representative, not just of women, but of the whole church. It was her risky and total consent to God's will that made her that representative. Her powerful commitment to nurture, enabling and interdependence rings out in her bold Magnificat:

> He has brought down monarchs from their thrones
> but the humble have been lifted high;
> the hungry he has satisfied with good things,
> the rich sent empty away.

Feeding children from her breasts, listening to their sounds to encourage their talk, waking up at night to their cries of hunger or pain, a mother finds a similarity between her task and God's but understands how much better a mother God is than she could ever be. Jesus shocked the traditionalists of all ages by referring to God as just such an intimate, caring parent. In discovering his mission, he freely accepted the crucifixion, telling us that the only way to salvation is to accept whatever suffering is the inevitable underside of our commitment to self and others.

Carl Jung finds in the life of Jesus a model for human development that has never been equaled: a man who could break with family and community expectations to follow his hard-won understanding of a unique mission not only on their behalf but on behalf of all human beings. Dom Sebastian Moore has attempted to relate the human psychology of Jesus to the theological tradition that has tried to explain his mission and crucifixion. As a human being without sin, Jesus came as a liberator of our desire, Moore claims. Undergoing all the developmental crises common to human nature, he was able to break through each inadequate, partial, identity to reach the desired union with the will of Abba, which was also his own deepest self, the self in touch with divine mystery. The crucifixion was the ultimate death to all but that self, not demanded by a vengeful God, but by the inability of those in power to receive this revelation of the need for all to undergo such transformation.

Even his disciples did not understand what he was giving them or asking of them. Yet in his acceptance of the crucifixion he did not seek, Jesus became, as Julian of Norwich realized, the perfect mothering figure. In the beautiful rendering by John of his last words to the disciples before the ascension, Jesus expressed his desire to draw all those who had been given to him upward into the presence of God. He spoke to them, he said, not as servants, but as friends. In all things, his words, his life, and his resurrection, Jesus was the protector and enabler of human growth, enduring rejection and even death so that all could become sharers of that life, fulfilling to perfection the human need for mothering.

In learning to love themselves so they can be sharers, mothers are often trying to be the kind of human person Jesus was and asked others to be. Mothers who are particularly aware of their vulnerability through the experiences of pregnancy, childbirth and child-raising tell us that they can become freer, more loving people only when they can turn their vulnerability away from victimization into equal sharing with others. When men experience their own vulnerability, it often makes them more sensitive to the vulnerability of others and to a similar sense of human interdependence. By themselves, vulnerability and interdependence are merely concepts, indicating the facts of our human experience. It is what we do with them that matters. If we integrate them into our continuous attempts to make sense of who we are and how we relate to others, we will grow as people who are both strong and compassionate, able to mother ourselves and one another wherever we meet.

6

Reconnecting Love and Truth

Recent research indicates that women's thinking is closely related to their sense of identity and their concern for relationships. A number of women philosophers stress the need to add caring to justice, thus posing an alternative to mainstream thinking and values. We are just beginning to see these differences and the hope they offer because hitherto women's development was simply assumed to be the same as men's, considered the "human" norm.

It is worth looking again at what this human norm was like. At its best, for example in the humane theory of Erik Erikson, it values responsible connections with others. He posits "caring" as the virtue of middle life, and the wisdom of old age as the ability to connect with oncoming generations in the face of death. Erikson says that his theory of the life cycle can be understood in terms of Ingmar Bergman's film *Wild Strawberries.* In that movie old Dr. Borg, who has cut himself off from his family and his past, revisits the earlier scenes and relationships of his life during a long automobile trip to Stockholm to receive a lifetime award as a distinguished elder physician. His patient daughter-in-law accompanies him on the trip, hoping to talk about the baby she is carrying and which his son wants her to abort. At first he tells her not to bother him; it's not his affair. By the end of a painful but illuminating journey, however, the old doctor has emerged from the cold self-preoccupation this response suggests, and will to some degree be a positive intermediary between his son and his daughter-in-law.

The focus of *Wild Strawberries* is on human interdependence and on the actively accepted, reintegrated memory of earlier dependence. Toward the end of the movie the old doctor is finally able to "see" his parents sitting in the distance together, waving happily at him. He has made at last the essential psychic journey back to relationship from his long separation. In *Wild Strawberries,* as in the best psychological theories, this transformation is an arduous creation, a virtuous achievement. With the broad acceptance of Erikson's theories, it is better understood today that all adults have to grow and change throughout the life cycle, and that such a journey represents healthy human development.

But words and theories are often masks for the reality they do not deal with in detail. And that is the case with theories of human development, which have been developed from studies of very limited groups of males. Dr. Borg learned to value relationships only after he had completed his professional career, beyond the world of work and dominant cultural values. Most American psychologists are far more pragmatic than Erikson and do not deal with the virtues of these later years. In addition, Erikson's background in the humanities has strongly affected his thinking, and he seems to have regularly incorporated the views of his artist wife into his theories.

In contrast, the best known study of human development in this country is the prestigious Grant Study, a heavily-funded and scientifically precise longitudinal research project that followed its subjects over much of their lives. The results, published in 1977 in George Vail-

lant's *Adaptation to Life: How the Best and the Brightest
Came of Age,* came with a *Wall Street Journal* blurb:
"Broadly and diversely applicable to aspects of the lives of
most of us."

The altruistic purpose of this study was to promote
mental health by discovering what kind of defense mechanisms worked best as adaptations to life. Its discussion of
such mechanisms and their importance is intelligent and
informative, but how can its findings apply to "most of
us," since it was carried out exclusively among well-
educated, successful, white men? It is startling, moreover,
to realize that its criteria for mental health were drawn
from the values of the men who were being studied: professional success and the ability to maintain some long-
term relationships, usually with a wife and children. No
women appear in the study except as "wives." And though
the author does not dwell on it, the research reveals a
surprising fact:

> The more successful the man, the more he feared
> women—not as individuals but as mythic be-
> ings. . . . While achieving their generative, "mas-
> culine" success, such men saw women in their
> innermost fantasies in a manner quite analogous
> to St. George viewing his dragon—as their most
> formidable opponent.

Vaillant quotes psychiatrist Robert Stoller in partial
explanation:

> Masculinity as we observe it in boys and men
> does not exist without the component of continu-
> ous push away from the mother, both literally in
> the first years of life and psychologically in the

development of character structure that forces
the inner mother down and out of awareness.

Men in our culture are thus encouraged to identify
themselves in opposition to women, mothers in particular.
No wonder women have a hard time seeing themselves
included in the Grant Study description of human development. The deep psychic processes revealed in this study,
reinforced by powerful institutions in our culture, have
long excluded the maternal from our public world. Seeking the roots of the American psyche, Erikson pointed to
the endless frontier, and the need of young men in particular to be able to move on. He cites the cowboy's loneliness
and inability to develop mature attachments as typical of
the adolescent nature of American male identity. This has
become clearer in recent years as women psychologists
have helped expose the strange cultural assumption that
individualistic, success-oriented standards of maturity are
"human."

Carol Gilligan's *In a Different Voice* reviewed the
dominant psychoanalytic theories and tried, "by using the
group left out in the construction of theory, to call attention to what is missing in its account." What was missing,
of course, was women's development, which does not proceed by way of achievement and separation but through
"relationships towards a maturity of interdependence."
Men and women view connection with others differently,
Gilligan observed, each fearing what the other does not—
men fearing connection, women separation. In this light,
the aggression dominating our culture appears "as the sig-
nal of a fracture of connection, the sign of a failure of relationship." With the rise of consciousness resulting from
the women's movement in general, this failure is more
obvious today.

Fortunately, evidence is beginning to mount that there is another approach to maturity which incorporates subjectivity into intellectual growth without succumbing to excessive individualism. Research into how women think reveals that for many the path involves just such a development to maturity. *Women's Ways of Knowing,* the important collaborative report by psychologists Mary Field Belenky, Blythe McVicker Clinchy, Nancy Rule Goldberger and Jill Mattuck Tarule, provides both insight and information into how women develop intellectually. The authors base their observations on a wide field of research, theories and insights as well as their collaborative reflections on their own research. Because they include thoughtful examinations of the way in which the family as well as schools have often hindered women's overall development, they have much to say to parents, teachers, and anyone with authority over others.

Belenky and her colleagues discovered five perspectives from which women tend to see and understand their world: silence, received knowledge, subjective knowledge, procedural knowledge and constructed knowledge. "Silence" suggests why the dominant metaphor of women for their own empowerment is "finding their voice." They use it to refer both to a sense of self and to knowledge. This choice in itself suggests the centrality of relationship for women. For unlike visual metaphors such as light, which imply both distance and separation between knower and known—common in science and philosophy—a voice implies a hearer, conversation and contact. Researchers tell us that little girls are much more likely than boys to choose telephones as toys. Computers too are seen and used differently by girls and boys, according to a 1989 *New York Times* report of a study of fifth grade students conducted by Dr. Lise Motherwell of MIT. Girls think of them as a person with whom they interact, while boys consider them simply as machines; "computers are often means for girls but ends for boys."

Not surprisingly, *Women's Ways of Knowing* finds that "silent" women were the most oppressed as children and the poorest as adults. These women see knowledge as something outside themselves, something that resides in authorities. They are the products of social disorganization; usually they have not been talked to or asked to talk as children. They find it difficult to describe themselves because they have not been told who they are. They also find it hard to say no to husbands who abuse them. If they are mothers, they cannot conceive of supporting their children's search for self and meaning. When the teacher complains about her child's behavior, a silent mother will not dream of asking the child what happened. She will simply punish her for disobeying the mandates of authority.

"Received" knowers also defer to authority, from whom they see right and wrong emerging in clear, dualistic terms. They lack the motivation and the ability to explore a child's mind empathetically or to be flexible in rule-giving. At best they lecture their children on what they have learned. Much of the dominant teaching from culture and church thus tends to reinforce immature development in mothers and their children.

Only when women discover that they have an "inner voice," when they begin to trust their own intuition, can they see that the world is not just given—and begin to respond to it. In the process they learn that they can think and make their own decisions, as some mothers discovered in our classes. This birth of the self can come at any age in women, Belenkey and her colleagues observed, even when earlier authorities have failed them.

Although trust in their own intuition often makes women belligerent and unable to hear others at first, the move into subjective knowledge is crucial. Yet subjective responses are not generally highly valued in school, business, or the church. They are often censured as selfish or sentimental responses, not "real thinking." Fear of women who are in this stage of development—whose reactions may be highly personal and idiosyncratic—accounts for much of the denigration of women's thinking as illogical and emotional. It is: tuning in to their inner voice, these women are seeking to integrate intuition and emotion into an overall perspective that will allow them to move beyond acceptance of external rules and received ideas. Though some women do remain stuck in this isolated, subjective stance, for most it is a necessary adaptation that prepares the ground for their further intellectual and social development.

When life situations present such women with dilemmas that they cannot solve with either received or subjective knowledge, they often begin the advance to procedural knowledge, the ability to gain information from outside sources that strengthens their own beliefs. The move is difficult, however, without support. It can be facilitated at college, where students are asked to learn new theories and methods, take responsibility for their opinions, and criticize others. Many women find debates and arguments uncongenial. They would much prefer to share stories rather than to make critical judgments. According to Belenky and her colleagues, teachers can best promote the development of women students if they help them see that they can use what they have learned to support their personal beliefs. Such students will thereby learn that truth must be sought and that the world is far more complicated than they supposed.

A constant theme of literature is the need to look beneath appearance to discover reality. Some women students who are helped through the procedural stage of learning will go on to excel in knowledge as mastery, but many will encounter history, science, literature and philosophy as ways to make the acquaintance of experiences and views very different from their own. That is why college can be such a liberating experience for women who return to the classroom after years at home with children.

Only when women seek to unite all these earlier perspectives, to find their own voice, not merely mimicking that of others, do they learn that all knowledge is constructed and can themselves become passionate and connected knowers. Belenky and her colleagues report:

> We observed a passion for knowing the self in the subjectivists and an excitement over the power of reason among procedural knowers, but we found that the opening of the mind and the heart to embrace the *world* was characteristic only of the women in the position of constructed knowledge.

Having learned to use the self as an instrument of understanding, such women "speak of integrating feeling and care into their work—using my mind to help people." Such care-givers—who are by no means all women—are not usually well paid or highly valued in our society. It is useful, therefore, to look at what women who have become mature, connected thinkers have to say about the importance of such care; their comments suggest some deficiencies in the thinking prevalent in our normative culture, particularly in the working world.

Assuming the reality of human interdependence, educational philosopher Nel Noddings calls "natural caring" the most basic human concern and the best school of moral discipline. She believes that human caring and the memory of being cared for are "the foundation of ethical response." Perhaps it is the foundation of artistic response as well. Artist Frederick Franck finds that when he uses a nursing mother as a model in his drawing classes, his students connect emotionally with their subject and it helps their work.

Noddings' analysis remains on the level of the natural. Indeed, she is suspicious of what she has seen when "supernatural" motives and approaches to care are used. She contrasts the caring relationship—always with a particular person in concrete circumstances—with an abstract "male" commitment to "spirit" that so often avoids the very interpersonal contact necessary for real care. The latter requires absorption in the one who needs caring, so that "the other's reality becomes a possibility for me." It must begin with seeing, hearing and feeling the other person's reality and language; only then will the care given really help the one who needs it rather than make the one giving it feel good. Response, not imposition, is at the core of the caring relation. The care-giver who knows what's good for you without asking is as ineffective as the lecturing mother or the overly righteous cleric.

Insisting that "the receptive mode is at the heart of human existence," Noddings sees the mother and child as her natural model of such care. All too much violence and destruction has gone on and been justified in the name of principle, she observes: "One might say that ethics has been discussed largely in the language of the father; in principles and propositions, in terms such as justification, fairness, justice. The mother's voice has been silent."

Sara Ruddick, another philosopher, has made that motherly voice audible in her study of maternal thinking and virtues. To be able even to conceive of such a study, she first had to overcome the discrepancy she herself experienced between the rich emotional and interpersonal mental life she led as a wife and mother, and the detached, abstract thinking which was all she could share with her socially valued philosopher colleagues. As a participant-observer among mothers, she was able to bring her philosophically trained mind to her analysis of mothering. Connecting her two worlds, she developed a concept of maternal thinking as an alternative to the abstract, divided approach dominant in her field as well as in the broader culture.

Ruddick does not idealize or sentimentalize mothers; she knows that many over-protect while others ignore and even abuse their children. It is not the goodness of mothers she describes but the thinking that accompanies their practice. Actual mothers, she points out, have the same relation to maternal practice as religious believers have to religious practice. This means there are wide variations. Ruddick distinguishes motherhood from mothering as I do, and insists that "maternal" is a social, not a biological category. She rejects the identification of womanhood with biological or adoptive mothering of particular children in families. Although maternal thinking arises out of actual child-caring practices, biological parenting is neither necessary nor sufficient.

Once again Dickens has already provided a model for understanding such a distinction. The best mother in his novels is not a woman, but the blacksmith Joe Gargery in *Great Expectations.* First he is a protector. The reader learns later that both Joe and his mother had been beaten by an alcoholic father when he was a child, and he had vowed for this reason never to use violence. This powerful man marries Pip's sister, who is a harsh, conformist care-

taker, in order to make up with his love for what the boy is
lacking. Next he is enabler, and one who can let go. He
sends Pip off to London, glad for the boy's opportunity,
enduring the young man's condescension for his unedu-
cated, provincial ways. But when everyone else has failed
the young man and he has almost died of brain fever, it is
Joe who is at Pip's bedside. His care helps Pip become an
adult at last, without illusions. The example makes clear
that, for Dickens, mothering is a human function, not for
women only. As his terrible rogue's gallery of weak, destructive mothers indicates, Dickens knew that self-knowledge and personal strength are essential if we are to
mother successfully.

It may be useful to look more closely at the world of
work in particular to illustrate what the invisibility of
women and the absence of caring in public life have
meant. A brief historical note should show how the present moment offers new opportunity despite its dangers
and divisions. As a review of papal social encyclicals would
confirm, modern economic structures have never paid
much attention to human needs. The values of our contemporary workplace developed without the benefit of human care, at the mercy of an aggressive bottom line men-
tality which, its apologists assured us, would produce the
greatest good for the greatest number. Because mothers
and nurturing values were both consigned to the private
sphere at the birth of nineteenth century English indus-
trialism, the public sphere was left wide open for unbri-
dled competition, land grabs, and the exploitation of people as so many units of production. Dickens' *Hard Times*
offers insight into the self-deceptive managerial mind
through the character of Bounderby, preacher of self-
reliance, who denies decent housing and any form of recre-
ation to his workers whom he thinks of simply as "hands."

He unconsciously projects his own desires on them, seeing any miserable worker who asks for justice as "wanting to be fed on turtle soup with a gold spoon."

After the Civil War, there were even fewer constraints on economic behavior in the United States, untempered by aesthetic or intellectual aristocracies, and with a seemingly endless frontier. Success and money opened most doors, and if one group didn't like the conditions imposed by railroad barons or mine owners, there were always new immigrants arriving who felt they had no alternative but to accept them. There were reformers, of course, who tried to point out the injustice of the working and living conditions endured by successive waves of newcomers to the United States—but even they usually ignored the even greater injustices practiced against native Americans and blacks. Many generations passed before there was a serious challenge to the power of those controlling working conditions, though the labor movement gradually gained a larger slice of the pie for those who were best organized.

Young women working in the mills shared the same long hours and harsh conditions as men. What made their situation different was that they were often not even "visible" as part of the work force; they would grow up and become the wives and mothers "workers" needed to give the men emotional support, maintain their homes, and raise their children. There is a personal thread to my interest in this still-recent history. At her stern father's insistence, the grandmother I am named for worked in a factory in Rhode Island as a child (from seven to fifteen), and in consequence was never able to attend more than a few years of school. I only knew her as a kind woman who was a good cook; she died when I was ten, and I have had to piece her story together. But my father and his sisters, who received the advantages of good schools and were able to go to college, occasionally mentioned her ignorance and the embarrassing remarks she made in public. A few years ago, when I went to a retirement home for nuns to visit her daughter, my aunt, who had had a distinguished career as professor of French and Russian, she confided to me how much her mother longed for an education. It was a realization she had only come to years later. "She used to beg me to teach her French and I just laughed. I know now how much it would have meant to her."

The great photographer of U.S. social conditions in the early twentieth century, Lewis Hine, has left us a poignant series of photographs of children working in dehumanized and dangerous conditions in Rhode Island in 1912, when he was associated with the National Child Labor Committee and the Consumers' League of Rhode Island. One photograph of "Card-Room Hands" in the Lonsdale mills shows a group of boys and girls from ten to fifteen; their intense eyes gaze directly at us, their expression serious beyond their years. But when the humanitarians who sponsored this publicity for the good of children described their reformist intentions, the young women had somehow disappeared. As one of the group described their goals, "The child was the carrier of tomorrow's hope whose innocence and freedom make him singularly receptive to education in rational, humane behavior. Protect him, nurture him, and in his manhood he would create that bright new world of the progressives' vision."

Naturally, I reflect on my grandmother's life. It is her eyes I see in the picture. She would escape the drudgery of the factory, but she could not learn what she so desperately wanted to. She too must have suffered from the inappropriate public remarks her children were embarrassed by. Her inability to become interdependent was part of a larger social context which depended on the work of women but gave them little public recognition.

Despite all the social changes since the turn of the century, including the women's movement, the kind of thinking that sees the workplace as purely male continues. Women's values are still considered abnormal in the workplace, and women themselves, including mothers, often come to accept the dominant cultural assumptions.

Torn between family and job obligations, many working mothers are deeply divided in their outlook, showing once again that women do not "naturally" think differently, as some might naively imagine. The experience of being excluded, invisible, and yet responsible has caused some of them to identify with those who are powerless, while others feel trapped in a dilemma. One study of career and family concerns by Barciauskas and Hull found that half the professional women questioned were not sure that they liked the Supreme Court's 1987 decision upholding a woman's right to job security after maternity leave. "It's wonderful for my daughter, but it would mess up our office," was a typical reaction of this group. The other half, however, especially those whose primary concern was for children, said that the workplace had an obligation to adjust to family needs.

Almost all the professional women in the study also believed that they were the ones ultimately responsible for the care and raising of their children. This perception —still our cultural norm, according to Nancy Chodorow in *The Reproduction of Mothering*—reminds us that society is still encouraging men to fit into the same individualistic assumptions assumed by the Grant study. Many of my male students seem to buy into the same process of understanding themselves in opposition to women, identi-

fying themselves through sports, drinking, driving and
sex, rather than learning what might be common to male
and female.

One might have hoped that religion, still so powerful
in this country, would endow the culture with that respect
for relationships so evident in the Bible, where God's concern for the people of Israel entails a comparable concern
on their part for widows, orphans, and even strangers. St.
Paul uses the powerful image of "the body of Christ" to
illustrate the interdependence of church members:

> Just as all these parts, though many, make one
> body, so it is with Christ. . . . The eye cannot say
> to the hand, "I do not need you," nor can the
> head say to the feet, "I do not need you." What is
> more, it is precisely the parts of the body that
> seem to be the weakest which are the indispens-
> able ones. . . . If one part is hurt, all parts are hurt
> with it. If one part is given special honor, all parts
> enjoy it (1 Cor 12:12–26).

Unfortunately, this inspiring vision of interdependence has been deeply undermined by the Cartesian understanding of mind and matter as separate realities,
which has dominated modern thought. In its words, of
course, the church challenges success as a goal in itself,
and certainly does not believe in treating people as objects. But its practice emphasizes law, its thinking sepa-
rates logic and emotion, and its teaching often divides
priests and people, heaven and earth. The absence of a
sense of connectedness produces an unintended but real
bias in regard to sex and gender that has distorted the
truth of the church's own teaching.

When the pope advocates human conditions for

workers, for instance, he seems to assume, like those Rhode Island reformers early in the century, that workers are men, and that this reform will enable their wives to stay home. But the phenomenon of women working outside the home is not simply a matter of temporary economic dislocation; such employment is a part of their human development and represents a significant contribution to the values of the common culture as well as to the economy. Neither the church nor the government should act as if the home is separate from the public sphere—they are thoroughly interconnected in the consciousness of those who move in and out of them—and only thinking that faces up to this changing reality can help, as the pope wishes, to improve the lives of workers.

Even some post-Vatican II thinking, although it springs from high ideals, reflects the divided, hierarchical approach that still characterizes so much church behavior, particularly in regard to gender differences. Trying to incorporate Freudian psychology into their evaluation of the maturity of seminarians, for example—an important task in these days of declining vocations to the priesthood —Fr. Vanasse, a distinguished Jesuit psychologist at the University of Louvain, reveals an unintended gender bias in his criteria. Having adopted a scale which sets up "two series of qualities describing the two essential pivots of every psychological structure: the Father and the Mother," he reports that the seminarians who participated in his research showed "tensions, therefore conflicts, in the sense of a need for acknowledgment and acceptance." He sees as immaturity "the prevalence in many priests of the mother image as the very often unconscious driving force in their behavior. . . . If he is truly to accede to the function of believing, the subject must accept the necessary loss of the primary object . . . the

Mother." In other words, just like the men in the Grant Study, the seminarian must come to accept the "higher" principles of law and justice represented by the Father.

According to J. Giles Milhaven:

> Thomas and other theologians ignored the wisdom growing from sexual love and pleasure . . . they ignored generally any wisdom coming from the ordinary love and pleasure of "common origin and sustenance," of living together in family, of eating day after day at the same table, as well as of making love.

In other words, he says that male theologians discounted all forms of knowing coming from family life, while the great women mystics derived their thinking primarily from this family experience. Only now, perhaps, are these women seen to be the modern thinkers they are. In their light, we see that the young seminarians expressing a need for acceptance might have been expressing a healthy need for human attachments as well as for a God with feminine as well as masculine attributes. To acknowledge such needs is to think clearly as human beings, and to be good priests they need to be good human beings first. Their testimony could be important for the church as a whole if we are to build communities that can attract and nourish priests who as whole human beings can relate to others. Telling seminarians to repress the maternal will only tend to form them in the same narrow maleness from which our culture is desperately trying to escape.

Let us return for a while to real mothers in order to pick up additional clues on how to overcome these hierarchies and divisions in our thinking and to promote caring in public as well as private life. Sara Ruddick's book illuminates the characteristic strengths of mothers' thinking and judging, which develop out of their practice of caring for children, and is governed by three main interests: to preserve their children, to help them grow, and to produce in them adults acceptable to their group. These interests seem loosely parallel to those I discovered in reviewing earlier cultural symbols of mothering; though Ruddick does not specifically include endurance, it is clearly implied in her overall vision of good mothering. It will be useful to analyze the virtues and shortcomings Ruddick sees in the thinking of mothers as they respond to their children's chief needs, and then reflect on their possible implications to our concerns as people and church.

Good mothering involves thinking, not just instinct or intuition. As a mother tries to balance the need of protecting her children with that of enabling their growth, she is all too apt to become overly anxious and exercise excessive control. The habit of thoughtful reflection can make a real difference in counteracting this trend:

> Though necessarily controlling in their acts, *re-flecting* mothers themselves identify rigid or excessive control as the likely defects of the very virtues they are required to practice. It is the identification of the liability as such, with its implication of the will to overcome it, which characterizes this aspect of maternal thought.

This was certainly true of the mothers in my classes. They were quick to point to their own failures, but even quicker to want to do better, if guilt and confusion did not leave them emotionally crippled. A sense of inadequacy seems inherent in the practice of mothering. A reflective mother has to be aware that she has not always been able to respond to children's real needs in their best interests. It is almost impossible to have a consistently accurate picture of a child who keeps changing every day, becoming a new person in an environment which is also changing and never completely under parental control or even observation. But to acknowledge gaps in understanding, to accept one's imperfection despite good intentions, is to acknowledge the human condition. When mothers can see and accept their own fallibility, perhaps errors of judgment in dealing with their own children, they can go on and use what they have continued to learn, can "hold" others, perhaps those who are not their biological children.

Catholics should find it natural to look to the human Mary as a model. The gospel suggests that she was disturbed to discover that her twelve year old son had stayed behind in the temple to talk with the rabbis. When he responded unexpectedly to her anxious question, however, she did not immediately tell him he was wrong but "pondered these things in her heart." From the evidence of scripture, she did not quite understand what he was doing even at the marriage of Cana, on the eve of his public life. She had faith in him and his goodness, so she asked him to save their host from embarrassment when the wine ran out. Continuing to reflect on her son's mission, she was prepared to stand by him when he was put to death by the legal and religious powers of the day. Later she helped support the frightened apostles until the Spirit came to strengthen them.

Sara Ruddick sees the virtues of the thinking that grows out of the attempt to preserve what is fragile—and which so often does not completely achieve its goal—as good humor and humility. She uses the definition of humility proposed by philosopher-novelist Iris Murdoch, for whom "Humility is not a peculiar habit of self-effacement, rather like having an inaudible voice; it is selfless respect for reality and one of the most difficult and central of virtues." Mary has always been known for her humility, but it has too often been interpreted as just such an "inaudible voice," as if she were one of the silent women, rather than the mature, interdependent thinker the Magnificat shows her to be. Perhaps the unexpected cheerfulness and humility of Pope John XXIII gives us a more contemporary insight into the virtues suitable for a mothering community. Kurt Klinger reports one of the stories the pope told which reveals both good humor and humility and has stuck in my memory:

> In the first private audience he had been granted, a newly appointed bishop complained to John XXIII that the added burden of his new office prevented him from sleeping. "Oh," said John compassionately, "the very same thing happened to me in the first few weeks of my pontificate, but then one day my guardian angel appeared to me in a daydream and whispered: 'Giovanni, don't take yourself so seriously.' And ever since then I've been able to sleep."

I have met many mothers whose lives reveal their ability to transform their failures and sufferings into preserving what is fragile in the lives of others with just such good humor and humility—in other words, who are connected thinkers and vulnerable sharers. A mother who was in her forties when she first joined one of my parenting classes is a good example. Angela had married young into a tightly-knit family from a different ethnic background than her own, moving into a house in which her husband's parents lived downstairs. When they had three children, her husband, who drank heavily, began to beat her regularly; instead of giving Angela support, her mother-in-law would harangue her for not being cooperative: "A wife's duty is to support her husband!"

Basically good-natured and optimistic, Angela is also a devout Catholic. But when her husband began to threaten the children with violence, despite her commitment to making the marriage work and her own sense of failure, she felt compelled to plan an escape. One night she and the children left quietly so that the in-laws would not stop them by force, leaving most of their possessions behind. Angela returned crestfallen to her mother's home and worked as a waitress, later as a restaurant manager, to support her three children.

Some years later she married again, and has remained with her second husband after seeing him through a successful recovery from drug abuse. Having survived the stress of her children's adolescence—one daughter went briefly to a reform school—Angela showed up in class already a passionate knower, eager to help others deal with family conflicts and substance-abuse problems. She probably knew more about the drug scene than most of the experts she met. One day she brought her daughter to class, a lovely young woman with a calm, happy four year old son. She was able to describe her stay in reform school as a valuable learning experience. She was on the best of terms with her mother, whom she obviously respected. Now that she has finished community college, Angela is working with a small support group she helped to form for the spouses of addicts.

Even more remarkable to me than her ability to flourish despite the potentially destructive experiences she had faced was the extraordinary care she had taken not to turn her children against their father, her first husband. She encouraged them to build relationships with him after he recovered from alcoholism. "I was bitter for a while, but I finally swallowed it. I knew it was better for the kids, and now I find out it was best for me, too." This tough, cheerful woman embodies just the virtues that provide an alternative to the values of mainstream culture.

Angela's story is typical of countless mothers who must deal with desperate conflicts for which neither school nor church has prepared them. At every stage they have to learn new thinking; they have to preserve and protect, but also to let go, to be open to change. Above all, they need to be able to tune in to the inner lives of their children, since, as Ruddick reminds us, the young often have no way of expressing their deepest experiences in words:

> A child is itself an "open structure" whose acts are irregular, unpredictable, often mysterious. A mother, in order to understand her child, must assume the existence of a conscious continuing person whose acts make sense in terms of perceptions and responses to a meaning-filled world. Who knows that her child's fantasies and thoughts are not only connected to the child's power to act, but often the only basis for her understanding of the child and for the child's self-understanding.

Only by combining the capacity of attention with the virtue of love, states Ruddick, can a mother respond authentically to the needs of a child; such "attentive love" to someone outside oneself implies a priority of personhood over action." Quoting Iris Murdoch, to whose development of Simone Weil's concept of "attention" she credits much of her own analysis, Ruddick states that the idea of "objective reality" itself "undergoes important modification when it is to be understood, not in relation to the world described by science, but in relation to the progressing life of a person." Here is a major clue to the kind of thinking that is concerned to enable people.

Such thinking is also essential to accurate perception, to the search for truth. As Murdoch points out, clear thought alone can never guarantee the accuracy of our views. Thought is only a part of life, and it is important that it be related to—not separated from—the rest of us, particularly our emotions and our interaction with others. Whether we call it original sin or self-interested projection, the evidence is that we fool ourselves in terms of our own desires. In her small but significant book *The Sovereignty of Good*, Murdoch criticizes the limits of the logical, verbal approaches to moral understanding taken by most of her philosophical colleagues, who are unconscious of their subjection to assumptions based on class, sex and race. Loving attention to others in everyday life, she stresses, is the most effective school of human morality. For the ego, the self-delusion that blocks awareness of their own motives—even among the best and the brightest—will also deceive the most brilliant moral theorists.

Murdoch's novels reveal how difficult it is to practice this respect for the reality of others. Her chief characters, mostly men, pursue their illusions repeatedly, passionately; some are slowly able to shed them only when literally dumped in the mud. As for Murdoch's women characters, all too often they cede their powers of independent observation to such men, and their abdication of power is as destructive as the men's assumption of it. In several of her novels (such as *Flight from the Enchanter* and *A Fairly Honourable Defeat*), magnetic, irresponsible men attract and destroy those who admire them. They themselves are out of touch with their own motives and often unable to enjoy life because their ability to dominate other people makes them cynical. Yet the world generally gives them its trust.

Murdoch suggests a very different kind of moral hero. In *The Sovereignty of Good* she proposes a mother-in-law (the butt of so many jokes) who does not really like her son's wife: she doesn't like her taste; perhaps the young woman is from a different class or ethnic background. But this mother—like mothers everywhere—wants her son to be happy. Over the years at family gatherings, she begins to change her mind as she observes the good though unfamiliar qualities in her daughter-in-law. In her willingness to withhold judgment and pay attention to her daughter-in-law, she stretches her mind and heart, coming to see her son's wife with respect as well as affection. Murdoch sees this mother-in-law's slow transformation in attitude and behavior as typical of the ordinary process of moral growth. It is quite different from assenting intellectually to the clear statement of a truth (love one another).

Real mothers are immersed in conditions which prompt such moral and intellectual growth, yet they are not often encouraged to develop or share their reflections in public. They must use their own eyes and judgment and not defer to the opinions of others when the good of their children is in question. The women philosophers I have cited think for all of us in much the same way. Weil, Murdoch, Ruddick and Noddings do not let custom or fashionable theories blind them to what they know on other grounds. Their writing reveals how destructive power over others in personal relationships can be, as well as its capacity to distort perception. That is why Murdoch stresses the danger of both power and powerlessness and

the need for encounters of all kinds that are mutually respectful. If we attend to them with humble, loving attention, we shall gradually be able to gain intimations of the
patient presence of good in all that is. Intellectual knowing
is always partial and related to our response to actual
things and people. The danger lies in abstraction that dis-
tances us from the complexities of reality and allows us to
excuse ourselves from dealing with *this* person in *this*
situation.

Murdoch's analysis helps us understand why ethical
behavior is largely absent from our public life. The absence of attention to relationships with genuine concern
for the good of all—their nurture, their enabling, their
ability to share—creates a real dilemma for mothers responsible for training children to enter it. If they follow
society's norms, can they help their children to act on values that conflict with that society? If they have trained
their children to accept prevalent norms as good, they are
often all but forced to support the aims of society even
when they contradict the values they hoped to impart.

Even when they are aware of this conflict of values,
mothers are often unable to resist the extraordinary pressures on them—to buy expensive toys at Christmas, to
make decisions as if success was the prime goal they held
out to their children. Ruddick suggests that the relative
powerlessness in the "real" world of women who seemed
powerful to their children when they were young may
account in great measure for the need we have encountered among successful men to repress the mother:

> Children confront and rely upon a powerful ma-
> ternal presence only to watch her become the
> powerless woman in front of the father, the
> teacher, the doctor, the judge, the landlord—the

world. A child's rageful disappointment in its powerless mother, combined with resentment and fear of her powerful will, may account for the matriphobia so widespread in our society as to seem normal.

She believes that our cultural attitudes can change only "when mothers insist on the inclusion of their values and experiences in the public world which children enter, when *they* determine what makes their children acceptable."

There is a central strand of tradition in the church which affirms and reinforces what the women philosophers I have cited are saying. It suggests that thinking rooted in a concern for relationship is—or should be—characteristic of all human beings, not only women, because it is rooted in our relationship to God as ground of our being. The doctrine of the Trinity stresses loving relationship at the center of the Godhead. The witness of mystics and theologians affirms that loving encounter with God enables people to pursue truth with the increasing humility and self-discipline such a search demands. A prayer from the sixteenth century *Sarum Primer* reveals just such an approach to learning:

God be in my head and in my understanding
God be in mine eyes and in my looking
God be in my mouth and in my speaking
God be in my heart and in my thinking

Such a prayer may sound unusual to our secular ears, but it would have been quite acceptable to John Cardinal Newman who continued to pursue and witness to the truth despite personal loss and trials. Illness and bereavement undercut any tendency he might have had to trust reason alone as a guide in life, for he thought that belief rested on the quality of our encounter with God, and it is this relationship which determines the orientation of our faith.

The idea of "truths" that are unchanging, outside of the natural and historical contexts of our discoveries about reality, are even more foreign to contemporary understanding than they were to Newman. Teilhard de Chardin's statement that "Faith has need of the whole truth" is a beacon to all people in the church, for it reminds us of the necessity of observing our corner of creation both critically and lovingly if we are to think more accurately about its creator, and take up our end of the relationship. It is right for people who are church to be both attached and objective. Our faith tells us that love and truth are unified. One does not rule out the other, but rather connects the rigorous search for truth with loving attention to the good of particular people and things.

In a public way, it asks us to work for institutions that will form others to pursue the truth lovingly: to clarify and direct reason away from mere self-interest or conformity, to see it rather as part of a collective effort. Such efforts would enable people to think about what they care about. If we are willing to encourage differences of opinion and build strong and honest relationships with those who hold them, we will be acting as a mothering people.

7

Spirituality in This World

If interpersonal relationships are our fundamental school of morality, relationship with nature is the basic school of our spirituality. This understanding is clear in the story told me by an English nun who had once taught physics at the college level. When I met her, she was in her fifties, and her passionate interest in a holistic approach to learning and growing had led her to learn foot massage. Her earlier training in the faith had been narrowly intellectual and out of contact with physical reality. She told me that physics had helped her see connections between matter and energy that kept her spiritual life from atrophy.

Physics taught her that life was not lived in the mind; it involved trial and error, push and pull, a constant learning through the experience of colliding against other psyches similarly embedded in matter. Still an active sister, she told me she was preparing herself for a different approach to mission in a modest way that reflected her new understanding. "People are often afraid of psychologists," she said, "but when I am massaging their feet they can talk openly to me without fear."

It has taken many of us raised in the pre-conciliar church a long time to reeducate ourselves to the possibility of such service to the spirit through the flesh, recalling that of Jesus washing the feet of his disciples at the last supper. His act seemed merely a gesture of humility to me when I attended parochial school; in different ways both the nuns and my parents contributed to my sense of living in a universe divided between sacred and secular, mind and body.

The nuns taught me how to parse sentences, how to write, how to be an intellectual achiever. They prepared many of us well to get ahead socially and at work, though we had a narrow sense of the society in which we lived. Citizens of Providence, Rhode Island, we never heard the name of Roger Williams mentioned as one who had put his life on the line for religious freedom. He was simply a Baptist, not one of ours. Mentally I felt part of a beleaguered, immigrant church even though "our" politicians were running the city and my own great-grandparents had lived in New England since before the Civil War.

The religious training we received directed us largely toward private devotion (which I loved) and a morality of clannishness and avoidance of evil (which I disliked but did not escape). It did not encourage independent thinking, but rather the dutiful reception of given truths. We were here, after all, to get through this "valley of tears"— a phrase used in a prayer that followed every mass—to make it to heaven as uncontaminated as possible.

I bought most of it. When the counselor at summer camp insisted on prying me away from Anne of Green Gables or Robin Hood to go on a nature walk, I was annoyed. This was a dubious Protestant occupation; they had to have something to make up for all the statues, stained glass windows and legends of saints they had so heedlessly thrown out, thus making religion a drab affair of nature and social responsibility. Catholics didn't trifle with such substitutes; we went for the real stuff: angels, rosaries, novenas, stations of the cross, holy pictures, suffering in silence and offering it up. We were in this world but not of it. No need to look at the leaves or grasses, as Father Cyprian had confidently told Felicitas in Mary Gordon's *The Company of Women.* That would be "womanish," not "orthodox."

In that comic novel Gordon recorded a profound change in sensibility among Catholics in the years since Vatican II. Many were seeking connections between their actual lives, work and faith in a far more complex natural and social world than they had envisioned in childhood. For Catholics of my era, perhaps the last, most difficult awareness is that all mind and spirit is rooted in matter.

In my case it was complicated and delayed by a different sort of influence from my parents. They had both gone to good "secular" colleges (still heavily Protestant in practice) and, having suffered discrimination themselves, had become passionately tolerant of the rights of others to hold different beliefs. If the church was out of this world, my parents were in it. They were wonderful dancers, gourmets, amateur musicians, travelers, theatergoers. Among my happiest memories are those of hanging over the banister (having sampled the food before) to hear the song and laughter when friends came over for parties.

I did not mind their disagreements with the nuns on tolerance, an unpopular virtue in Catholic school. But I was mortified by my mother's insistence that we avoid communion when "germs" were making their rounds. A dedicated reader of manuals on health and child-rearing, she put some sort of metal armor on our hands so we could not suck our thumbs; I could never have my throat blessed on St. Blaise's day because of the danger of infection. My mother did not find "nature" any more reliable than the nuns did; only "experts" and scientists could be fully trusted.

A mechanical engineer, my father too believed in "progress." He was convinced we could order and control our emotions. He really believed that reason was the most powerful force in people's lives, despite the evidence around him which often left him discouraged—especially with his family. He attended mass regularly, but I believe his faith rested to a large extent on stoicism and an accurate knowledge of his own intellectual limits. "If the best man who ever lived was put to death for seeking the truth, who am I to think I understand truth better?"

Only much later did I come to understand that my mother's reliance on experts and my father's insistence that we should all "Think!" (he kept this IBM motto on his desk) were not idiosyncratic, personal choices: hers the classic tendency of American mothers to follow "experts," his the male acceptance of the enlightenment belief in progress and machinery that Henry Adams had portrayed as the dominant American myth.

And so both my religious and my home education reinforced my own temperamental inclination to separate mind from matter, and to treat the latter, including my own body, as a kind of poor relative. I know now how inaccurate such a view of the world is. I cannot read the elegant essays of biologist Lewis Thomas without being convinced of human relatedness to living matter at every level from cell to universe. Thought rises from life, he insists, not the other way round. The writings of scientifically trained observers like Rachel Carson and Chet Raymo have shown me how the religious imagination can inhabit a personal scientific pursuit of nature whose accurate discoveries evoke awe and wonder. Today I accept the thesis of Thomas Berry—who calls himself a "geologian," one who interprets the wisdom of the earth—that the earth is our primary, living teacher whose lessons we must attend.

The reason I can hear these prophets of the convergence of science and religion today, however, is largely because they confirm connections that first became real to me through my experience as a wife and mother. In traditional civilizations sex was closely related to ideas of the sacred, and generating life was a cosmic act. But even in the secularized 1950s here in the United States, conceiving and bearing children involved mysterious, demanding encounters with hitherto unsuspected reality.

Pregnancy and birthing forced me, almost for the first time, to pay attention to the welfare of my body for serious reasons. Instead of indulging my appetite or dressing for display, I learned about nutrition, yogic breathing, and natural childbirth. Neither the food industry nor my doctor was helpful in the 1950s, but I read Dick Grantly Read and did my exercises with determination. As I prepared to give birth, my body became less an object to me, something I dressed up and moved around, and more the vehicle of my own existence and that of the potential new life within me.

The awakening and acceptance of their sexual embodiment was conveyed to me with great power by the women I described in *Sex: Female; Religion: Catholic.* Pregnancy as a significant milestone for women's self-understanding—their bodies, themselves—was also clear in the mothering classes. Young women became far more aware of the need for exercise and nutrition and trained for birth as if it were the Olympic event of their lives. It probably was, not only for the mothers but for many of the fathers. Several men attended La Maze classes with their wives and were present at births. Three different fathers confessed that their presence at birthing had been one of the emotional high-points of their lives. They tended to speak of the "miracle" of birth more than mothers, though both recounted feelings of awe. Yet this experience was different from their earlier conceptions of awe because it was the fruition of pleasure and love as well as the result of strenuous human cooperation. To these parents, nature was the source or channel of spirit, neither separate from it nor below it.

Their grasp of this relationship of spirit to nature had been captured in words centuries before by the clear-eyed English mystic Julian of Norwich, who spoke of God's presence in our lowliest bodily functions. One of her more famous images is that of the body opening like a purse in time of necessity as a sign of God's gracious care. It is an image to which parents can easily relate. As Carol Ochs writes, they know that

> the decentering of self achieved through asceticism can be accomplished as well by true devotion, which is first and foremost physical caring. In caring for their infants, mothers don't seek to mortify their sensitivities—they simply know that babies must be diapered and that infants who spit up must be cleaned. They count the action as no great spiritual accomplishment. By merely doing what must be done, their spiritual development proceeds without pride and without strain —it gracefully unfolds.

The spontaneous way my students gave testimony to the spiritual significance of birth also caused me to reflect that public discussion of pregnancy, birth and nursing was comparatively recent in middle class culture. A grandmother reminded us that the word "pregnant" could not be spoken on the radio when she was growing up, nor could a respectable woman attend a public affair in "that condition." Several older mothers were amazed that younger women wanted to be conscious during birth or to have their husbands present. "I was petrified by all the stories I'd heard of unendurable pain during delivery, and my doctor was eager to put me under anesthesia," said one, while another recalled: "I had twilight sleep; it knocked me out and they handed me a pink bundle the next day."

During our sessions on childbirth I also discovered that the increasing desire for consciousness and participation on the mother's (and father's) part was a cause of conflict between them and standard medical practice. Prospective parents would often seek out natural forms of childbirth or the services of midwives only to discover that many physicians called such care "substandard" and sought to limit it. Parents who tried these alternatives, however, were enthusiastic, not just because they cost so much less but because "midwives think about you and your family, not just the baby. They counsel you ahead, give you nutritional advice, massage mothers, talk to them and let their husbands assist." One woman reported proudly that her husband cut the umbilical cord. "The birth was treated as a sacred thing in our lives."

Of course babies sometimes need to be born in hospitals with the care of doctors. I was Rh-negative, and at the time this posed a serious threat to babies' lives. My youngest needed a transfusion immediately after birth, and I value the care that let him leave the hospital in good shape in nine days. But most births are, as women feel them to be, natural events. A number of mothers in our classes had read about Dr. Leboyer's practice of non-violent birth, in

which hospital lights are dimmed and voices are lowered
as the baby emerges, and the newborn is not slapped, but
given a gentle bath in warm water to begin this new life.
Yet they found it hard to convince their doctors to use
such methods.

Anthropologist Emily Martin helped me understand
the cultural significance of this tug-of-war between
mothers and doctors. Her research suggests that women
have a different conception of their bodies than most of
the professionals who deliver their babies and write text-
books on how to do it. She discovered that the majority of
the women under medical care at Johns Hopkins whom
she interviewed felt to some degree alienated from their
bodies because of the medical interpretations they had
internalized. "Your self is separate from your body" was a
typical comment. Martin found that women experience
this separation with special intensity in Caesarian births,
the most extreme medical intrusion into childbirth.

She studied metaphors in standard medical texts relating to menstruation, birthing and menopause. Invariably they suggested that the mainstream medical understanding of birthing closely resembled that of industrial
production. Menstruation and menopause were seen as
failures in production, breakdowns in a system designed to
produce a healthy product. Such understanding, Martin
believes, led many doctors to want to control production,
increasing their desire to immobilize women through
Caesarian sections.

She discovered that when women were encouraged to
continue talking about the same bodily processes after
their initial claims of separation from them, they began to
use more positive metaphors. Menstruation, for example,
became a sign of womanhood and something shared
among women. Childbirth became a cooperative exercise,

one that could give a woman who was not too drugged a feeling of riding the whirlwind or being a channel of the life force. A number of women in menopause differed sharply with the image of failure and breakdown used by the doctors, claiming that for them menopause brought a period of new energy and independence, a fresh and exciting stage in their lives. Research such as Martin's shows that presumably objective medical attitudes are often only cultural interpretations of a reality that could be seen quite differently if women's experience were consulted.

There is a long history in western culture behind the alienation of women from their bodies and the attempts of scientists to control nature. It may ultimately be rooted in men's fear of death and their tendency to equate women with death and chance. In Greek mythology both Fortune, who smiles and then abandons you, and the Fates, who snip the cord of life, are portrayed as women. Joseph Campbell believes that the fear of women and the mystery of their motherhood have been for the male as fearful and mysterious as the world of nature itself.

Yet chance and death are the bedrock realities of the human condition, inherent in creation. The desire to break with the feminine, then, equated with nature, implies a desire to escape from reality, to create a mental break between matter and spirit that runs counter to experience. As western culture became increasingly fascinated with scientific discovery, technology aimed at controlling and even replacing nature, a Faustian ambition that identified the human at its highest in *opposition* to nature.

In such a brief summary I am inevitably oversimplifying complex cultural developments, but even this overview may be useful in suggesting how the ancient world's respect for Mother Earth gave way to a spirit of conquest and domination over the earth and other people. Not long ago we were taught to applaud this history as the triumph of "man"; we are now able to see its sinister underside, and to understand how the identification of the earth as a nurturing mother links women's history and ecological history.

In *The Death of Nature* Carolyn Merchant traces a continuing reverence for the earth in all pre-historic pagan religions through historic Roman times. In his *Natural History*, for example, Pliny warned those who would mine the land for their own enrichment not to disturb our "sacred parent." This sense of the earth as mother, combined with the organic sense of the universe as a whole, persisted in the west until the renaissance and acted to some extent as a moral restraint on behavior.

The discoveries of Copernicus, however, began a shift in focus from the earth as organism to the earth as machine. Different images of the earth rendered it more passive and open to exploitation. A number of feminist writers have pointed to the rape and torture imagery in Francis Bacon, the pioneer apologist of modern science. This is how he described the experimental method to King James: "For you have but to follow and as it were hound nature in her wanderings, and you will be able when you like to lead and drive her afterward to that same place again." The biology and medicine of the time used similar gender symbolism to reconceptualize nature and render it suitable for dissection and experimentation as well as for the exploitation of its resources.

These troubling images, of course, do not sum up the scientific enterprise, whose quest for objective truth about reality is ultimately related to the religious quest. But they do reveal the often unconscious projection of human superiority and male supremacy that would shape and tarnish the findings of many scientists as well as profoundly affect the course of western economic and political development.

Sadly, the official church sidelined itself as a moral critic at just this time when it was most needed. Concentrated on preserving its "authority" in the face of scientific discoveries by forcing Galileo to repudiate his observations, it lost its chance to inform this new thinking with moral imagination and its traditional language of awe and praise. Unfortunately, Christian witness was further diluted by angry divisions between Protestants and Catholics, with each side identifying with competing national monarchs.

This meant that, as the age of exploration began, the unifying, sacramental view of life had largely lost its force in the west. Powerful nations would export the same contradictory drives they had at home: soldiers and missionaries would go forth together to seek souls and gold. The moral blindness of such conquests would encourage European immigrants to the Americas to believe that they were promoting lofty goals in dominating those they saw as merely "natural," hence sub-human, creatures. The slave trade was part of the same process that saw native Americans driven from their land, fought almost to extinction, and finally herded into reservations which kept them poor and segregated. European-born settlers could not conceive of an encounter with the traditional religions of Africans and native Americans, which might have rekindled an earlier sense of awe before the natural forces now being plundered. Mother Earth was either sentimentalized or thought of as merely a naive Indian superstition.

We all appreciate the advances of science and technology that enable us to live longer, to travel and communicate in ways that our ancestors would have believed possible only through magic or miracle. But it is blindness not to recognize the underside of our "progress," often based on the objectification of nature. Poet John Allman finds our situation illuminated by some of the best science fiction, which depicts what he calls a "motherless creation," one that substitutes "male science" for female nurture. Frankenstein inhabits a world without mothers and the doctor is a creator who does nothing to further the happiness of his creation. In *The Island of Dr. Moreau*, H.G. Wells presents an isolated scientist who lures visitors to his vivisectionist experiments and is indifferent to his children's pain. Allman sees a common factor in these examples:

> It is curious . . . that so many of the mad scientists we find in science fiction are engaged in creating beings without the agency of a woman or of a nurturing maternal principle. The absence of that maternal element has been and is characteristic of science in the modern world. It is partly the product of a belief that objective detachment from the natural world is a prerequisite for the practice of science.

The science fiction Allman analyzes mirrors a profound lack of trust in life itself. One could argue, he says,

> that what is missing is a benevolent God, that the mad/male/scientist has locked out of the picture a God he cannot trust. One could also argue that this scientist father is fashioning himself after a patriarchal Creator who Himself never had much use for women.

The extent of motherless creation is all too visible in our world today. Human abuse of air, water, land, and forests are pushing these systems over thresholds beyond which they cannot sustain life. In 1987 The Worldwatch Institute reported that ours is the first generation "to be faced with decisions that will determine whether the earth our children inherit will be inhabitable." Daily contamination of the atmosphere and mass extinction of plant and animal species have led us to the brink of catastrophic climatic change. The report concluded that "The very notion of progress begs for redefinition in light of the intolerable consequences of its pursuit."

When the mothers I spoke of in Chapter 2 stayed after class to bemoan the weakness of good in the community, they had nothing so horrifying in mind as the death of the planet. They were concerned about their children's use of drugs and the inability of church and school to reach their imaginations with power similar to that of rock music and advertising. One of those mothers, however, has since formed a citizens' group to organize against local environmental destruction. At first she thought she was just fighting another unnecessary shopping mall which would increase traffic and air pollution. It turned out that the site contained two toxic dumping grounds that had been overlooked, and that, to carry out their project, the developers were prepared to remove a hill whose slopes held a cemetery for local African-Americans dating from the Civil War era. Next to this proposed mall is the dump, now higher than the neighboring hill, which must be closed this year by state law. Yet no substitute deposit for the garbage has yet been found, and every other method of disposal so far considered will spew more carcinogens into the air.

Almost all communities have similar problems. Anyone who shops for food knows of other chemical hazards. More and more people buy bottled water and seek out organic produce. It is clearly not in our interest to pursue every technological change possible. Perhaps only a crisis of the present proportions could have awakened us to the need for a more respectful attitude to the earth.

"Science" is not the culprit; mathematical biophysicist Evelyn Fox Keller helps us see that this objectifying and distancing of nature is only one way of doing science, even though it still dominates scientific investigation. In her *Reflections on Gender and Science*, Keller demonstrates that the network of gender associations and assumptions characteristic of the language of science are, in fact, a present deterrent to the basic scientific search for reliable knowledge about nature and the impulse to share it.

Insisting that their approach is totally impersonal and objective, scientists often remain unaware of their own motives and the projections they impose onto their theories. Science, Keller observes, has been dominated by white, western, middle-class men with a particular ideal of masculinity. The world they view as "object" bears the peculiar subjectivity of their isolation from it. An opposition between love and knowledge has been part of their development and their science. She applies to their thinking the observation of child psychologist Piaget: thought which is not conscious of itself is a prey to perpetual confusion between the objective and subjective. Piaget insists that it is necessary to use subjectivity consciously in order to achieve a more effective objectivity. Such an approach, whether in a child, a mother, or a scientist, recognizes that differences between self and other are opportunities for insight and kinship.

Keller cites the scientific term "laws of nature" as an example of researchers' myopia. It is a political term, not a scientific one, she claims, and its use reveals the desire to turn regularity into law, preferably one unified law. Her own research into slime mold aggregation suggested that theories which assume hierarchical organization and the need for leaders tend to become accepted very quickly and to blind researchers to other possibilities that might explain their data just as well. She saw that spontaneous, collective reactions to changing environmental factors could account for the same phenomena, but they did not fit into the pre-conceptions of most researchers.

Neither did the approach of Nobel Prize winner Barbara McClintock to her research. This geneticist and cytologist claimed that a "feeling for the organism" one observes reveals a much more complex order in nature than humans can imagine. Keller tells us that McClintock saw nature as truly prodigal: "There's no such thing as a central dogma into which everything will fit." Indeed, McClintock's growth as a scientist was characterized by her discovery of difference, which she found everywhere, and believed to be an end in itself.

Moreover, she saw this very difference as an invitation to a kind of understanding that preserves the value of the individual. No two plants are exactly alike. You have to get to know them to discover this, however. McClintock did. She developed a kinship with her plants from the time they were seedlings. And in the process she gradually became able to distinguish chromosomes she had not been able to see before. Instead of "objective" distance, her approach stressed empathy; it demanded the loving attention of a participant observer, a vulnerable sharer. Her relationship to the plant world was similar to that required for successful caring among people. It rested on a deep sense of identification with plants in order to distinguish and support difference among them. This view reveals a natural world that is globally interdependent and resourceful, able to respond to environment and change without "leaders." It made McClintock dubious about Watson and Crick's doctrine of DNA because it explained too much, was too hierarchical, and went in only one direction. Yet it is their assumptions, not hers, which have dominated further investigations.

Nevertheless, hers match what much new scientific thinking reveals about our relation to natural phenomena. These sciences of complexity show that in evolutionary developments, from blood vessels to rivers to galaxies, all life is concerned with relationships as means rather than objects as ends. Increasingly, this sense of relatedness has marked my own maturing inner sense of who I am and where I am. Martin Buber, the great contemporary Jewish philosopher, insisted that "all life is meeting," and he made a point of including trees as well as human beings as "others" and not "objects."

Despite my childhood scorn for nature walks, such a consciousness has become stronger in me, in regard not just to trees but also to wind, water, stars and birds. I cannot walk by a salt pond in Rhode Island without being overcome by the pleasure of the company: extended families of swallows perch on telephone wires and suddenly rise in circling sweeps only to descend on the neighbor's roof. Robins, mockingbirds and red-winged blackbirds in the trees and marshes compete with seagulls complaining over the pond. Cormorants and swans scavenge near the shore; wild roses and honeysuckle lend their decaying sweetness to the salt air. Almost every hour the wind comes from a different direction, changing the aspect and color of the water, just as the tide constantly changes its level. Every night the sunset varies, just as the moon and stars do. Yet there is a soothing regularity in all these changes that signify growth, life and death.

Perhaps because I have myself participated in the cycle over time, grown older, seen children grow and leave, experienced the death of friends and family members, I now feel myself a participating observer in this show, not a detached viewer. If only I had had a small sense of this when I was nine or ten, I might have learned the things I would like so much to know now—to be able to see at a glance the long history in a rock, to understand how plants and sea have shaped each other, instead of simply admiring their appearance. From this perspective science seems a pursuit deeply compatible with religious belief in a creator. How can we know the creator if not by the way this world has been made?

Because I see the patient, loving energy squandered in the prodigal production of so many possible creatures, I do not fear the dark or the moaning sound of the wind at night, though its voice is eerie beyond the power of words. Despite earthquakes and tornadoes, I have trust in the way this world works. I see that as each thing dies, it is replaced by others. Now I understand better what Virgil called the tears of things, the necessary limitation and inevitable mortality of all created beings, beautiful and beloved. But these tears, although filled with grief, are nevertheless tears of joy. They spring from wonder. They manifest a trust in nature that psychologist Erik Erikson calls the essential foundation of any human growth, love or morality. It is equally the ground of any spiritual development.

As in medieval poetry and theology, a tree is a tree and also a reminder of the tree of life and the tree of the cross. Reality is itself and also a rich reminder of the energy that created it. A spirituality that overvalues asceticism is liable to miss this rich source of spirituality that comes from loving and living in our natural habitat. Avoiding the world, we may be avoiding the very source of life, the challenge to our mind and imagination that provides us with asceticism in a human setting: in a family, a community, a natural environment.

It is right and important that we celebrate our bodies, to begin with. Reading Whitman's "The Body Electric," or his insightful poem in which a young woman—forced into corsets and covered from head to toe—looks appreciatively and longingly from her window at naked male bathers on the shore, I am persuaded of the rightness of such celebration and am appalled to think how recently women have had the opportunity to share it. For so long the bodies of women were covered and corseted so that they could not enjoy the natural world as men could. Yet paradoxically, in art they were almost always uncovered for public gaze. The female nude, woman in the abstract as an erotic object, was always widely available. Only very recently, with the new freedom of thought spurred by the women's movement, have we been able to see the human cost of becoming such an object. In Margaret Atwood's *The Handmaid's Tale,* which describes a world where powerful men are again firmly in charge, confining and using women's bodies, the handmaid narrator observes an odalisque, in which a naked woman lies stretched out on a sofa for visual delectation, and points out how unbearingly boring such a position and a role are to the woman involved.

Finding their voices as they are freer to use their bodies, women bring a new sense of reality into male-female relationships and a new sense of relationship to their encounters, from sex to sports. When women become actors instead of objects of sexual desire, both men and women are freer to discover sensual joy (rather than conquest and submission) as an important part of loving. When men help with the children, both can discover the delight, rather than just the duty, involved in living with children. When men and women help with selecting and preparing food, ordinary meals may become a movable feast.

Duty is not nearly so powerful a force as joy. Learning to respect all other things and people because we share some identity with them increases our ability to enjoy the differences among them. As this becomes habitual in our private lives, we will be strongly motivated to widen that sense of respect by transforming our economic and political world. If we know that the animal butchered to provide meat for our meal has been raised in miserable conditions, we will want to put pressure on the cattle industry and think about adopting a different diet. Francis Moore Lappé has called to our attention the connection between decisions to cut down rain forests (encouraging the greenhouse effect), the inability to produce enough food for all the people on the planet, and the increasing consumption of meat in the world's richest countries. If we know that the clothes we wear were made by underpaid sweatshop workers, we cannot enjoy wearing them. Such transformative awareness develops instinctively when feeling and attention are brought to all our encounters with reality. We then recognize the truth of Marie Augusta Neal's contention that altruism in economic and political affairs is in our own best interest.

Just as ordinary joy and wonder come to daily life partly through our sense of relationship with all things and people, so they enter our spiritual life as an integral part of existence. Ochs' description of ordinary motherhood is a basic corrective to other-worldly spirituality:

> Mothering is a process of total caring—physical, emotional, psychological, and intellectual. In response to the demands made by the infant, the

mother must de-center the self and focus on the
needs of her child. She helps form the child by
"holding"—a term that describes several kinds
of nurturing care. She must also know when to let
go, when that becomes appropriate for the
child's development. Learning to value the child
as belonging to itself and learning to love without
possessing are major spiritual achievements. As a
mother involved in teaching a child all its first
skills she learns to focus on achievements and not
on mistakes. Her knowledge of her infant can be
achieved only by empathetic identification. By
learning to know her infant in this way she becomes familiar with a kind of knowing that is central to spirituality.

It is a way of knowing that has a long tradition in the
church, a sense of sacramentalism which sees all things
both as themselves and as signs of God's love. The assumption that grown men and women needed loving nurtur-
ance in order to grow spiritually was widespread in the
twelfth century, for example. The image of Jesus as
mother was powerful, too, reflecting a sacramental attitude toward the world in all its cultural manifestations,
from cathedrals to romances, according to Caroline
Bynum. Abbots felt the need to show affection to those
under their care. Aelred of Rievaulx is reported to have
died confessing to his monks, "I love you all as earnestly as
a mother does her sons." The spirituality which flourished
among twelfth century Cistercian monks stressed the
motherhood of God and Jesus, drawing on such Old Testament references as Isaiah 49:1, where God's care for us is
compared to that of a mother for the child in her womb or
at her breast, or Isaiah 66:13, in which the Lord asserts

that "As a mother comforts her son, so will I myself comfort you."

But as we have seen, male theologians discounted such feminine knowing because it was too physical. It could not, by definition, be spiritual. "Knowing" was impossible through suckling a child at the breast or the embrace of love. Only in our time is it possible for male thinkers to question such hierarchical divisions and find that the physical, "womanly" thinking unifies body and spirit as they are unified in human experience. Is not touching and other physical means of knowing "the most precious mutual awareness of each other that the family has?" asks Giles Milhaven.

> Tactile are not merely the eating and drinking together, giving suck, playing with the baby and having sex, which are described in the women's "visions." (For traditional thought, touch is the sensation involved in orgasm, swallowing and sating hunger and thirst.) But touch is central, too, to supporting the baby taking its first steps, clothing the child, embracing mutely the bereaved, holding the ill person's hand, sleeping together, the playful wrestle of children, the adult hug of reunion after long separation. To contradict Thomas: are we not in these experiences "more knowing" than usually? The depth and extent of tactile knowing can also make an act more evil, as in the slap or brutal kick delivered, or in rape.

A far different, other-worldly spirituality is fostered by the idea that the church is separate from and superior to the secular world, one that does not help unite body and spirit in every encounter. Our present-day celebration of the eucharist reflects the loss of a sense of the sacramental unity of matter and spirit. Yet theology and tradition tell us that the eucharist is our thanksgiving to God for life, that it is rooted in nature and social relationships. Jesus initiated the sacrament at a meal with his friends, and the first ecclesial celebrations were communal feasts in recognition of the revelation that bread, wine, and food—fruit of the vine, work of human hands—when shared among believers, could memorialize and make present the sacrifice of Christ. Our task is to connect those elements from an earlier tradition with our attitude to science so that we can live joyfully in this real, sacramental world.

Mothers (and others) who prepare Thanksgiving dinners or seders have a more or less conscious sense of what is involved. Such occasions need not be empty formalities; they can be truly feasts of love, remembering missing relatives and friends, welcoming strangers. When eaten at such a feast, lamb becomes something more than meat, but pizza or tacos can take on significance, too. The strange mixture of elements we always find in human celebrations are signs of the sacred, reminders of social ties, reflections of the tensions we find in our own wavering between faith and doubt. The seder scene in Woody Allen's *Crimes and Misdemeanors* captures some of this tension in the contradictory attitudes of those seated around the table, some quick to deny the presence of God in the world because of its patent injustice, others willing to choose him over truth. Neither group seems able to connect God with this world.

We need to face the Genesis task anew, building the peaceable kingdom within ourselves and in our corner of the world, as we are, even though we are all to some degree desensitized by pre-conceptions about matter and spirit, notions of what is male and female, and attitudes to sexuality that are detached from the rest of our experience. Flannery O'Connor shows us that we can proceed even if we have been miseducated in this process of incarnating spirit in our own bodies and sexuality. Her semi-autobiographical short story "Temple of the Holy Ghost" tells of a southern Catholic girl on the verge of adolescence. Shocked at the mindless boy-chasing conversation and behavior of her older girl cousins, who are forever polishing their nails, she cannot imagine a future for herself as a female. But although she mostly resents the training she receives from the nuns, she has at least gained from them an intellectual understanding that her body is the temple of the Holy Ghost. When her cousins return home from the county fair and tell her about a hermaphrodite "freak" they have seen, she later dreams she hears him talking: "God made me this way and I don't dispute it. . . . God done this to me and I praise him. . . . Raise yourself up. A temple of the Holy Ghost. You! . . . God's spirit has a dwelling in you, don't you know? A temple of God is a holy thing." She wakes up aware that God's love extends much further than she had imagined.

This revelation enables the girl to accept her budding sexuality even though she will be a "freak," a woman who is an independent thinker and an artist. At the end of the story, having attended benediction at the convent, she prays: "Help me not to be so mean." As the girl looks out the window of the car, God's energy become palpable in the mysterious world she inhabits: "The sun was a huge red ball like an elevated Host drenched in blood, and when it sank out of sight, it left a line in the sky like a red clay road hanging over the trees."

Physics professor and naturalist Chet Raymo conveys a comparable vision. Watching meteorites on a summer evening, he discovers "a universe of wonderful dimension, complexity, and beauty." Though the "narrowly anthropomorphic forms of traditional theology" in the church of his childhood were inadequate for his intellectual development, Raymo brings to his passionate search for meaning in all natural phenomena the sense of mystery he gained from the liturgy and the lives of the saints.

Raymo asks again the question of St. Lawrence, "Whom should I adore, the Creator or the creature?" The creation is here, he concludes, and as a passionate participant-observer, he praises its mysteries. He does not claim too much for his findings, though they illuminate the possibilities of science as a fully human search:

> I sought the burning bush and did not find it. But
> I found the honeysuckle and the fuchsia, and I
> found the gorse and the heather. When I called
> out for the Absolute, I was answered by the wind.
> If it was God's voice in the wind, then I heard it.

On a broader scale, Thomas Berry foresees the convergence of science and faith when both see that

> the natural world is not simply object, a usable
> thing, an inert being awaiting its destiny to be
> exploited by humans. It is subject as well as object,
> the maternal source from which we emerge
> into being as earthlings. It is the life-giving nourishment
> of our physical, emotional, aesthetic,
> moral and religious existence; indeed, it is the
> larger sacred community to which we belong.

If you have come with me this far, perhaps you sense what I do. Not only are people around the world groping for a new human identity, but for the first time millions have become aware that they live in a universe in which every part is already attracted to every other and moves because of that attraction. Forces like gravity, which used to be given a purely mechanical meaning, can now be interpreted by physicists as "attraction." Our era is one of such enormous potential change on the planetary scale that it brings to mind the breakup of the middle ages.

At that time the discovery that the earth was not the center of the universe, around which the sun moved, tended to destroy people's confidence that individual, earth and heaven were related, that there was a great chain of being from atom to God. As we have seen, the age of exploration and the birth of science was unfortunately also the age of conquest and individualism. Today the discovery that human beings are literally part of the fiery explosion that began the ongoing creation of the universe restores the connection of all things along with their distinctness, particularly the creative potential of each unique human being. The ancient wisdom that earth is our mother, we find to our delight, turns out to have been right; it is our life-support system, our common holding environment. The old divided terms no longer apply: jobs versus clean air or water, animals versus human beings. The new story of science shows that their survival is interrelated.

Flannery O'Connor used Teilhard de Chardin's phrase "Everything that rises must converge" as the title for yet another of her harsh revelations of human weakness that is saved by staying where it can still be reached by insight and grace. As believers, each of us may well be in a position each day similar to that of Teilhard when he offered his remarkable mass on the world. Finding himself in the desert without the materials needed to celebrate mass, the visionary priest-paeleontologist used the world itself as his altar: "Since once again, Lord—in the steppes of Asia—I have neither bread, nor wine, nor altar, I will raise myself beyond these symbols, up to the pure majesty of the real itself; I, your priest, will make the whole earth my altar and on it will offer you all the labours and sufferings of the world." His prayer moves from the rising sun to "the ocean of humanity," seeing the toil of men and women everywhere as "this all-embracing host which your whole creation, moved by your magnetism, offers you at this dawn of a new day."

Are we not each day in his position, offering our attempts to grow along with those of all that which is also growing and changing as he continues the mass on the world:

> This bread, our toil, is of itself, I know, but an immense fragmentation; this wine, our pain, is no more, I know, than a draught that dissolves. Yet in the very depths of this formless mass you have implanted—and this I am sure of, for I sense it— a desire, irresistible, hallowing, which makes us cry out, believer and unbeliever alike: "Lord, make us one."

8

Building Community
Through Communication

If we have caught some of Teilhard's vision of the connectedness of all things, it is easier to understand the urgency of developing intellectual and spiritual dialogue instead of indulging in zero-sum debates. Such two-way conversation would strengthen and transform the church in its ability to offer counter-cultural values, but this approach requires a mutual discipline we have not taken seriously, the kind practiced by nurturing families. It is time to analyze what that involves and see if it is feasible for the family that is church.

Here we are, whatever our age, trying afresh to relate to others in the world God made us part of. It's a little like being born again, but it's not a once-and-for-all experience—it keeps on happening. And, of course, we're not quite starting over. We had no say about our genetic inheritance, the family, ethnic and national group into which we were placed, even the religion to which we were first introduced. As adults, we must take a more conscious position regarding the selves we are, through reflection on our experience. Even if we can affirm lovingly most of what we have received, it is still our obligation to continue to make sense of what we have learned from all our encounters with others.

155

To do so, we must pay more conscious attention to the way in which we take in information as well as the way we express ourselves, listening, learning to develop our authentic voice as we hear those of others—not letting our office, our role, or our rule speak instead of us. Communication is a difficult skill when we practice it with people who differ from us in language, culture and religion, or with those who are relatively powerless. Yet we have probably built up habits that make it more difficult still. Since early childhood we have instinctively constructed defenses against people who disagree with us, misunderstand us, or seem unfair. And sometimes these very defenses make it harder to interact with others in such a way that both they and we are better for the exchange. The question is: Now that we are adults, can we gain insight into our style of communication and even get control of it? Once again, the habits of parents with children suggest that it is possible; they even suggest the outlines of a useful strategy. The relearning I have seen among parents seems equally suitable for the family that is church.

Family therapists stress the importance of good communication in building self-esteem in children and parents, and the presence of such self-esteem as the prerequisite for straight conversation. Mothers who nurture infants know very well that their children's mental and spiritual well-being is tied to their physical and emotional development. That is why they take seriously what they say even to babies, trying to show love through eye and body contact so as to stimulate loving response. And that is just the beginning of the family conversation necessary to foster that trust in the world that is the foundation of all human growth and morality. Therapists tell us that good communication is the largest single factor in determining what happens to people in life and what kinds of relationships they will be able to have with others.

But parents are never able to communicate all the love they might wish to. Even if we leave out extreme cases of child abuse—which are far more frequent than society wishes to acknowledge—we all have personal knowledge of vulnerable young people being deeply hurt in more subtle, less physical ways. When parents are immature, under extreme pressure, or out of touch with their own feelings, despite good intentions they pass on their failure to communicate. People in most families, however, if conditions are not overwhelming, can gradually improve their skills in building mutual understanding and support. Virginia Satir's popular handbook on family communication, *Peoplemaking*, shows us how such reeducation works.

Satir begins by describing the kind of conflict-producing responses she has invariably seen in troubled families. She has found that when problems arise, family members who feel threatened tend to adopt one of four defensive stances which block communication: they blame someone else, cave in to the other person, talk about the problem in abstract terms, or just change the subject. Needless to say, none of these styles of response helps the people involved or deals with the problems they face.

Many of us grew up believing in the happy endings of old-time Hollywood movies; we had to learn that problems are inherent in family life. People who expect problems to occur can more easily use them as opportunities; despite past failures, we all can learn to deal with them to some extent. Reading Satir helped me realize that I made things difficult for my family by not expecting problems, and often reverted to the bad habit, gained in growing up with a handy younger sister, of blaming others. In my child-raising years I remember using all four of those communication styles that don't work: I blamed and I caved in; I dealt intellectually with emotional issues, and sometimes I danced around them. It took me a long time to see this and even longer to start changing. I had to feel secure enough to lower my own defenses, to admit that I didn't know it all, to believe that having limitations wasn't tragic. It is still a struggle, but worth it. I really trust my family, but even now I sometimes find it hard to talk and act on that trust. In my case it often demands a tighter lip and more creative listening. Earlier, it meant overcoming the habit of keeping things from the children, a practice that always backfired.

Improved communication necessarily involves greater self-understanding. Satir points out that you can't talk honestly to others if you don't accept your own feelings, and that the ability to accept them can only flourish in an atmosphere of tolerance and support, an open community with flexible rules. So the process is circular. It's getting started that's difficult; the "straight communication" Satir advocates is in conflict with the predictable tendency to protect ourselves during family fights. Openness is especially hard to achieve when conflicts reflect deep differences across generational lines, or are heightened by pressure from school authorities or police. Yet face to face communication in which all sides really listen and hear is essential. If you assume, just because you're supposedly adult and respectable, that you always know what is right for your children even before you've listened to them, you may not ever get to know them—or yourself. You will certainly not be able to create that world of trust that Erikson sees as the foundation for children's later learning and loving.

The ordinary collisions of parent and child in daily life afford ample opportunities for dialogue, but it is often difficult for parents to gain the necessary objectivity or self-knowledge to use them constructively. So much of what we do is below the level of consciousness that we often behave in ways guaranteed to produce results we do not intend. It is much easier to observe this in others—our own parents or teachers, for instance. That is why I have students analyze the quality of parenting in stories we read together before trying to reflect on their own.

Satir provides simple exercises with which to begin; for instance, monitoring the family conversation at the dinner table for its emotional rather than its verbal content. "Please pass the potatoes" can convey polite hunger or murderous rage. Satir's exercises also help parents see that the rules they think are understood by all family members may not be. One mother in my class complained for weeks about how impossibly messy her teenage children were, never cleaning their clothes or their rooms. One day she simply asked them what the rules of the house were; she found out they had no idea. Taking a deep breath, she asked them what they thought they should be. They began to make suggestions, and before long she and they worked out a few they could live with. Though their rooms were still not as clean as she might have wished, she was glad to lower her housekeeping standards in exchange for more relaxed, cooperative relations with her children.

Ironically, both the psychologist and the local priest, when they try to teach family members about their responsibilities, often overlook the need to learn how to work as this mother did for goals common to parents and children.

The psychologist tends to stress children's developmental needs while the priest is likely to emphasize the parents' obligation to provide discipline. It is not that they are wrong, but they show little conception of the importance for children and grownups to connect, to share their inner feelings and hopes, and to develop relationships that can create self-discipline within an atmosphere of trust, the basis of community living.

In the mothering classes, we tried to connect parents' and children's development as it occurs in reality, stressing the opportunity for growth that life offers to both through their relationship. Psychologist Maureen Haberer, who developed and taught those classes with me, also developed a parenting practicum that focused on communication; it was designed to help parents get to know their children and their own parenting styles more accurately. Attending those sessions, I saw parents learn how to help young children develop self-discipline through the kind of close, loving attention to communication between them that always accompanies good mothering.

Maureen developed her techniques from such diverse sources as Virginia Axline's play therapy, Carl Roger's interpersonal counseling style, and Dr. Arthur Kraft's listening techniques. Her success, however, depended largely on her own educated guidance of parents who reported weekly on their sessions with an individual child, usually one who was in some kind of trouble.

This practicum began in response to an anxious nursing student who was about to drop her studies because her eight year old son had terrible stomachaches that kept him out of school. On inspiration, Maureen suggested she spend a half-hour alone with the boy every night from 7 to 7:30, during which he would decide what they would do. She was to provide materials like clay, paint and dolls, which would permit him to express his feelings indirectly, and she was to be absolutely faithful to the schedule, not interrupting it even to answer the phone.

Less than two weeks after she began these regular sessions, the mother reported that the boy's stomachaches began to disappear and his resistance to school stopped. A few weeks later he said, "Mom, I feel kind of bad. Daddy's downstairs all by himself. I want to spend the time with him tonight."

Seeing how well this worked, Maureen decided to adapt the approach for a group. They too would have play sessions with one child once a week, and stick to the time without fail, using rules and materials she first shared with them. They were to let the child guide the activity; they were not to interfere or lead. Nor were they to comment on the quality of the child's art-work, for that would be a distraction from the main point, expressing feeling. The children could do anything short of physical violence or the destruction of someone else's property.

Parents who took this practicum were usually afraid at the outset that such permissiveness would spill over into their child's daily behavior. It almost never did, but when it happened, a quick reminder usually sufficed: "Oh no, that's OK in play time, not during the rest of the week." But parents had to mean it when they said: "You can do anything and say anything you want." If they broke the promise, they were shaking that most important principle, trust. At the same time, parents had to be firm, since some children were expert manipulators, starting new paintings just before the end of the session and yelling "I'm not finished!" The rules had to hold for both.

The experience of one five year old bully is illuminating. He tore up the daycare center while his mother attended class. He had picked up the vocabulary of a dockworker, largely from his father, and began to use this language more and more at home, distressing the mother. In order to counter the father's severe parenting, she had been bending over backward to protect him, and the boy was confused.

Maureen advised her that she would have to let him say anything he wanted in the play session without flinching, gasping, or showing any dismay. In the first session he began to use his worst words and kept looking at his mother. She calmly repeated them, and he began to scold her: "You're not supposed to say that." She knew that by joining him, by saying this one word, she was giving him permission to continue. Every week, no matter what else he was doing, he would spend most of the half hour spewing out a constant stream of dirty words. About the fourth week he ran to her between sessions and said: "Mommy, I want to say some bad words. Is it Thursday yet?" She said "No, it's only Tuesday; you've got two days to go." "O.K." he sighed, and he held it in and saved it for Thursday. Given the freedom and permission to let go within limits was teaching the boy to control himself.

About the end of the seventh week, as they got to the end of the period, she said: "We've only got a few minutes left."

"Oh, I forgot to say the bad words!"

"You've got two minutes left."

He rattled them off as fast as he could, and that was the last time he used them. The mother kept up the play sessions on her own for two years after the class, and the boy continued to become happier and more outgoing. Maturation alone was a factor, but the mother's affirmation of the child was undoubtedly important. It meant: "I love you just as you are, whatever you do and whatever you fail to do. I love you just because you are." The love of parents who see their real needs and hopes is protective and nurturing to children. It fulfills the first, essential requirement of all good mothering, building the foundation of a trusting, creative identity. Reaching the child with that love requires the kind of attention and skill on the part of parents that is really a moral discipline. But parents are not usually trained to listen much, even with their ears, and this listening calls for an awareness of body language, facial gestures, and indirect expression through paintings and manipulation of dolls. Parents need to listen with their hearts and all their senses. Only then can they learn to interpret what they see and hear so they can come to know their children more accurately than anyone else, and be capable of enabling as well as nurturing them. The point is equally applicable to anyone dealing with children. Some of those in the practicum were caretakers, teachers, or simply neighbors; the sessions were as instructive and valid for them as for biological parents. To make sure they were equally valuable for the children, Maureen used to insist that the participants make a date to see them in a few months, and to keep up the contact for several years at least. Like Mary Catherine Bateson, she also saw the value to these adults of relating to a real live child.

In Maureen's weekly groups some parents spoke of discovering a child's unexpected anger, expressed once by a boy who repeatedly used his boy puppet to hit a mommy puppet. At other times the discoveries were more positive. One of the first fathers who participated, for example, was a man in his late forties who had had a heart attack and was forced to change jobs. Because his wife was working, Steve came in to get help in dealing with their youngest child, five year old Marian. After the very first play session he was elated:

> I can't believe what I saw in that half-hour. I feel
> so bad I didn't know this when my older children
> were growing. I used to watch them playing in
> their rooms or the living room and all I could
> think of was, "O my God, if they'd only keep
> quiet. And I hope they clean up the mess."

Steve reported that he had watched Marian for the whole half-hour. In that short span of time he saw her create, design and solve problems, work through difficulties, express emotions, and then take responsibility for cleaning up. "I can't believe how creative she was. Maybe all children are." After his series of play sessions with his daughter, this man, who had been foreman of a large auto plant, decided to study for a new career as a teenage counselor.

Other parents discovered that they were not as democratic as they believed. One woman's older son used his half-hour to play parent, and spent the time saying, "Now you do this!" He would then walk around, shake his head and scold. In the same mother's second half-hour with her younger son, the experience was different: the boy spent the whole time asking her what to do. Since one of the rules was: No suggestions, no hints, dead silence if necessary, this went on for several weeks.

This mother finally realized that both children were telling her the same thing: she was very directive. "I had no idea!" she exclaimed. If someone had tried to tell her, she wouldn't have believed it, but when she experienced the fruit of her behavior, she was motivated to change.

The parents in these sessions were learning to practice a style of parenting that goes against the American grain, neither forcing nor hurrying their children's development, but finding out who they were and what they really needed. The great psychologist of childhood, Jean Piaget, whose educational theories were based on painstaking observation of children of different ages, used to talk about the "American question." When he lectured to general audiences in the United States about his findings —that free exploration by children was the primary prerequisite for any learning on their part, and that no amount of intellectual drilling or verbal information could be retained by children if they were not at the developmental stage to use it—he would still get the inevitable question: "How can I help my child move to the next stage?" Piaget used to insist that children's organic, intellectual and moral development could best occur when they were allowed to operate freely in an atmosphere of trust, but American parents continued to believe more in external stimulation and control.

Neither we nor our children can completely control our destinies. We are each born with certain possibilities and certain limitations, unique from birth, with definite temperaments that precede the actual formation of personality. Any parents with more than one child know this from experience. Yet they may not vary their style of parenting from one to another or even think they should. Such inflexibility, however, based on inattention and undue deference to outside experts, deprives them of the greatest adventure they, and only they, can have: getting to know their children well enough to help shape a future in keeping with their greatest potential. In the process, parents will get to know themselves better and gain invaluable feedback on their weaknesses.

Like a human family, the church today is badly divided; depending on their upbringing, its people have different conceptions of what is central to the faith and what are only culturally conditioned externals. If we are to build a genuine community, we will all need to work at improved communication and become more knowledgeable about human relationships. Institutional decisions made during the Second Vatican Council encouraged communication at many levels as part of decision-making processes in the church. This inevitably encouraged an outpouring of long-repressed differences of opinion and even some ill-advised initiatives, which in turn convinced some of those in authority to believe that the restoration of law is the only way to preserve tradition. Such leaders do not seem to realize that in placing emphasis on authority and a hierarchical approach to communication, they are out of touch with the patristic image of Mother Church, an egalitarian, spirit-filled community respecting and encouraging differences, and out of keeping, as well, with the church family John XXIII envisioned as a people sharing decision-making with one another in order to be just and caring in their use of the earth's limited resources.

If divisions are to some degree inevitable in both family and church, the key questions are: How can we live with them in honesty and harmony? How can we use them creatively as opportunities for growth? We all know of tragedies caused when differences are allowed to harden; some families stay divided, and some even cut off members. In the world of my grandfather, those who married outside the Irish Catholic group—in my area, this might mean with French-Canadian Catholics; in others, with Italian or Polish Catholics—were cut off from the community. The families of the bride and groom simply did not talk to each other.

When such separations occur in families, each side tends to exaggerate the faults of the other. It's hard to get Uncle Harry's point of view or understand why Aunt Alice left. Yet when they do not remain in contact, the whole family suffers, especially the children. The family that continues to invite Uncle Harry to holiday dinners despite his negative comments and bad jokes may discover that the children love him. Visiting Aunt Alice may be just the outlet an independent daughter needs to make her own way in the world and still stay in touch with the family. The extensions are wider when family groups include members representing different classes, or different ethnic and religious backgrounds. Creating community in a wider family calls for greater tolerance and perhaps forbearance as well as the gradual acquisition of more communication skills, but it is also an ideal way to nurture personal growth.

Church leaders, of course, do not intentionally desire to exclude any particular groups, but many fail to appreciate how easily the church community in practice mirrors the limitations, the housing patterns, the prejudices of the wider society. Publicized controversies have forced us all to recognize that Hispanics, blacks, and women feel ignored or under-represented in the decision-making of both church and state. Parents who switch from a bullying to a placating style in response to these groups offer no helpful model in this situation; the point is not to make some politically astute appointments, or to participate in some local festival—important and overdue as such gestures may be—but to realize that the church cannot become the family God wishes it to be unless its feast of plenty is genuinely shared by all.

The temptation to exclusion is more powerful in the institutional church when the issue seems to be a matter of fidelity to truth. Tolerance is then apt to be seen as watering down the faith, and those who are raising new questions, or arguing for the importance of rethinking time-worn formulas, will at first be regarded as enemies. When we are deeply convinced of something, we all find it much too easy to adopt a simplistic approach in which those who oppose our "truth" are clearly promoting falsehood. But trying to see and speak the truth is a creative and lifelong endeavor to grasp and express it a little more adequately. The necessity of ongoing conversation in the church is highlighted by Teilhard de Chardin's phrase: "Faith has need of the whole truth." None of us can truly grasp reality in its fullness. If we believe in truth as a power capable of moving minds and changing societies, we are obliged to struggle to understand and speak it as accurately as we can. In a family dispute I cannot say that I speak the truth but my husband or son does not. It is the same in regard to church differences: each has some truth to contribute to the whole.

We all try to tell the truth but often, perhaps unconsciously, we leave out something that might reflect badly on us. Carl Jung warns that it is far more destructive to lie to ourselves than to others; in the latter case, we at least know what we are doing. We all have mechanisms for avoiding such knowing, like the successful men in Vaillant's study who repressed "the mother" in themselves as the price of success. The possibility of truthful observation is directly related to our degree of consciousness and our level of maturity. Am I so emotionally insecure that I must be completely right and cannot see the validity of another position?

The church, of course, will survive its divisions; the point is to limit individual pain and the loss for all that separations produce. In the past, when educational opportunity was far more limited, it was much easier to repress differences, control communication channels, and isolate persistent critics. The "success" of this policy, however, has meant a serious deprivation, leaving even many loyal Catholics to continue to think of the church as "them," an external power to be obeyed, not a family in which they have a role to play. If today's church does not help its very different members to talk to one another and hear what they are saying, it will suffer from the same limitations that families undergo when they cut off Uncle Harry or refuse to visit Aunt Alice. Blaming others, caving in to power, and intellectualizing or ignoring questions are just as useless in the church as in a family. They tend to smother emerging meaning, which can only be developed by thoughtful questioning within an atmosphere of trust.

Clearly, the kind of communication that helps to nurture and enable families has something to teach the church family. Most parents are willing to listen to almost anything from a young child whose face shows love and admiration a good deal of the time. But when children are old enough to begin creating their own lives, the process is more painful on both sides. Teenagers frequently believe they have learned everything their parents have to teach; they've heard it all too often. They are extra hard on their parents, perhaps unfair, because at this difficult time their growth partly depends on their ability to separate from parents.

Yet the ability of parents to bear criticism from their older children and still stick around to support them is what psychologist Robert Kegan finds to be their essential task; they must provide the necessary "holding environment" older children need as they try to work through this difficult period of separation. Of course, it is very hard on parents not to feel crushed or repudiated when they are being contradicted by the very children who used to think them good and powerful. Many feel they have failed, maybe even wasted many years in their lives.

The ability to hear the truth of a child's criticism at any age is to gain in the practice of virtue. It is also to come to know oneself more accurately, and Carol Ochs reminds us that this has its costs:

> In the course of raising her children, the loving mother must allow for the possibility that her children will despise her. She must gradually dis-illusion them so that their idealization of her and their belief in her power and magic will disap-pear. Her children must finally see her as she is and come to recognize their own strengths.

Surely this same process of enduring feedback which is painful is essential to a church who is, as Karl Rahner reminds us, not only a holy mother but a church of sinners as well. She above all has need to hear the whole truth. She wants to disillusion her children in her own perfection in order to enable them to serve God.

This ability to live in tension with different answers to basic questions is the necessary school of moral maturation for all of us in the church. After all, religion is intended to assist people to make sense of their lives within an overall commitment to God's loving presence in the world and in others. But religion cannot do it for us. Like a good earthly mother, it must enable us to do it ourselves, and then trust us enough to let go.

Many church leaders find it difficult to foster such enabling and letting go because, in the face of different positions on a number of issues, they believe that there is one truth which should be clearly presented so that "the little ones" will not be confused. This approach rests on the assumption that truth is already possessed and understood, which is quite different from the psychological approach to truth as something we begin to see more accurately as we respond consciously to our experience. Of course, a central thread of that experience is our faith as mediated by the church community, but this is always seen in conjunction with the need to exercise our own conscience. Perhaps we have all lost sight of the fact that the church is both rooted in this-worldly realities—it has need of buildings, organization, wine, oil, etc.—and is permanently called to be an exodus community, trusting in what the Lord will make available on our route. Like parents, believers cannot know the future, and there are as many dangers in trying to control it completely as in failing to plan for the difficulties ahead. Abraham is the common father to all three great monotheistic religions of the west, because he responded to God's summons and went out into the unknown.

Service to the whole truth, therefore, should lead those holding authority in the church to hear the view of others who seem to be overturning traditional positions. They may provide the unexpected inspiration that will enable us to enter the future. The usual accusation against power is that it corrupts; my experience tells me that even when it does not corrupt in the sense of encouraging greed or the desire for domination, it nevertheless distorts the truth by diminishing it. I am not encouraging a superficial relativism, nor do I believe that all opinions are of equal value. But the speed with which some rush to judgment, or even threaten excommunication, is a sign of insecurity which only weakens authority in the church. Most Catholics are uninterested in the professional theological debate on the meaning of infallibility, and remain content with their faith in Christ's promise to remain with the church for all time. They know, often through rueful awareness of their own mistakes as parents, what an impossible burden it is to be regarded as all-knowing by those who are totally dependent on them, and can understand that good church authority, like good parenting, means working for an end to dependency. If the concept of infallibility is to retain any utility, it will presume ongoing two-way communication in a church which practices no exclusion.

That it is necessary to listen to the faithful in order to discover a truth that is wider, deeper, and perhaps different than some church leaders believe has a long tradition in the church. Just before the First Vatican Council, when Rome was intent to state its powers in monarchical terms, Cardinal Newman published his study of the Arian controversy under the title "On Consulting the Faithful in Matters of Faith." As I mentioned in Chapter 2, Newman saw this process as the traditional method for establishing truth in the church, one that placed the individual conscience in healthy tension with church officials responsible for preserving doctrine.

Newman saw infallibility as something belonging to the witness of the whole church. Among other things, the witness of women today could give very important feedback to church leaders on their mistaken notion that maleness rather than humanity or the ability to parent is essential for ordination to the priesthood. As Dom Helder Camara once said when asked if women could be priests, "I am not a theologian; but if God could make a woman the mother of his Son, I see no problem with women becoming priests." This is only one of the many questions dividing the church at the moment which cry out for constructive conversation.

If this and other divisions in the church motivate us to

become more patient listeners, there is apt to be less lecturing of others and a greater sharing of stories. Some do not yet even have the self-confidence to realize that they have something worth sharing with the larger community, but find it less threatening to tell their individual or group stories than to challenge experts or present abstract ideas to authority figures. Despite our lack of a common culture, family stories still help to shape identities influenced by the values they stress. Sometimes such stories strengthen and root young family members; at others they limit them. Sometimes they concentrate on the special qualities of sons, while making daughters feel less special. Other stories tell children that they never do things properly, just like Uncle Ed who never made good. But good family stories find a place for black sheep as well as kissing cousins. My mother used to tell me that I laughed like "cousin Elizabeth who never got a man." Like all oral tradition, family stories are open to reinterpretation and retelling; my unchanged laugh recurs in different, more positive stories today.

A Mother Church would strive to nurture and enable the expression of all, but particularly the silent, who are often the most oppressed. I was impressed with Mary Belenky's report on sessions she has been holding with women from poor rural families in Vermont who as children had almost no opportunity for communication outside the family. They had little self-esteem, indeed little sense of self. Being heard by attentive listeners and then being asked questions which triggered further reflection gradually led these women to realize that they had, in fact, been thinking all along; many found that they were creative problem solvers. Looking back on their experience, they began to tell stories which were so powerful that, when they heard them replayed on tapes, they were astonished. This practice in story-telling helped many to go on to speak up and deal with abusive situations that formerly seemed beyond them. Interestingly enough, at the beginning of these sessions the problem had been the women's fear of the psychologists' authority. Only when the latter devised a collaborative style of leadership in the groups did the women begin to open up—another lesson for those who wish to become good listeners in order to evoke the voices of those who have not yet realized that they have something to say.

As we become more sensitive to the stories we hear and those we ourselves tell, we will pay closer attention to the language in which we tell them. Many parents initially rely on language which is merely directive, discouraging questions, not realizing how this also discourages response. Surely the language we use in our stories will be different, reflecting our identity as vulnerable sharers observing and responding to the great mystery of being.

There is, I believe, a strong corollary between the American over-emphasis on individualism and the difficulty we have in communicating freely with different kinds of people, particularly dependents. The defensive stances of parents that prevent dialogue with children seem triggered by a fear of encroachment similar to the engulfment young people fear from adults. Because they have not themselves been nurtured to be self-directed, such defensive parents—as well as bosses, teachers, and pastors—cannot seem to open themselves to the vulnerability required of sharers.

It is possible to learn to be more open, however, and it has great rewards. As we have seen, receiving feedback helped parents become aware of how they actually talked, and whether or not they unintentionally conveyed mixed messages. I remember some unpleasant feedback I received in a class training us to work with volunteers. Told to do a complicated task fast in our group, I rushed to achieve the goal; I did not spend time consulting the others, but simply tried to persuade them. It was sobering to be criticized for being task-oriented, but it was true: I had been educated that way. In these sessions I learned that being sensitive to those you work with is at least as important as the work.

Listening to others, we also discover that people have very different styles of thinking and talking. If we are prone to talk in abstractions, it is hard to make sense out of the rambling, concrete stories which are the staple of others' conversations. I remember a campus minister at college who worked quite effectively for many fine causes but was impatient with the concerns students brought to her. "If only people didn't come in to talk about their private lives all the time," she confessed to me in frustration, "I could get somewhere."

On the whole, women prefer to use concrete language, rooted in experience, descriptive and non-judgmental. Perhaps it is their traditional responsibility for home, food and children that leaves many of them uncomfortable with abstract reasoning. They tend to dislike debate, prefer to share stories, and have difficulty in arriving at those "clear ideas" dear to many college professors.

Of course, concrete language is not specific to women. The traditional African education in morality, for example, in contrast with the European list of do's and don't's, was practical teaching in how to behave to one's father, mother, grandparents, and other members of the kinship group, paternal or maternal. In other words, language and conduct were taught within a context of relationships. As Jomo Kenyatta describes the moral education of the traditional Kikuyu, it stressed the immediate business of living, not abstract principle or science. Revealingly, European missionaries sometimes complained that African students were hopeless when it came to understanding morality, while the Africans often found the missionaries inhuman.

Such feedback suggests the intellectualist, disembodied attitude to morality long characteristic of western Christianity. Liberation theology, too, has enlarged our understanding by its method of beginning with an analysis of the social and economic oppression in the surrounding society. A number of recent official documents suggest the church is already learning from these new sources that its ability to see, hear and talk to those in other cultures needs correction. Madeleine L'Engle stresses the importance of such enlightened reconnection:

> Let us be thoroughly human, learning from our mistakes, keeping open minds, acknowledging our flaws and going on from there, not toward sterile perfection but toward thorough humanness. And that implies a willingness to ask questions, to let go old answers, to live with a paradox of contradictions. Such an attitude to language and behavior is rooted in our biblical tradition.

Both Old and New Testaments are rich in sensory language, images and stories that appeal to the whole person, not just the mind. It remains the best kind of language, the kind good teachers encourage students to write. When George Orwell railed against the aridity of abstractions in "Politics and the English Language," he turned to Ecclesiastes with its sensory images for examples of good expression. Jesus, too, preferred story-telling and homely metaphors to what we call theology.

Our words and styles of conversation, of course, are rooted in our attitudes to self and others, and so is the symbolism we use in liturgy. We need to look more closely at liturgical practices; we are often unaware that some symbols convey the sense of hierarchy and separation which alienates rather than connects. At one of the hearings conducted by the U.S. bishops before the 1976 Call to Action conference, I was struck by the testimony of a Spanish-American woman, who first passed around a statue of a pregnant Mary she had made in ceramics class:

> I have always wanted to see a statue like this because I can identify with a Blessed Mother more than a Blessed Virgin because I am a married woman. This is the Blessed Mother pregnant, expecting the Baby Jesus. . . . I had a poor image of myself as a mother and as being married because so much emphasis was put just on the Blessed Virgin, something so far out of my reach I could never be like her.
>
> I could not identify with celibate clergy or nuns either. It was hard for me to live a Christian life when I could find no examples like me. But how can there be a universal church if the root of the tree that is to give fruit is not a priority within the church?

Certain symbols unintentionally exclude people, suggest that some vocations are "higher" than others, or that the church does not love all her children equally. Last year I visited a sister teaching in a midwestern seminary, the only woman on the faculty. She told me that when the seminarians she had helped train were ordained, they marched up to a dais with the bishop and other priests, raised high above the congregation. They were then told to lift their arms even higher over the heads of the congregation. She felt that the message coming through to the people was that the newly ordained had ascended to a higher realm, had been placed *over* them. When the ceremony was over, my friend went up to each new priest and encircled him in her arms. "I wanted them to feel that we were *related*," she said, "that we stood on the same ground."

Other symbols can include people. I think of the powerful effect a few changes in the marriage mass of a young friend made upon me and others present to witness the wedding. First we were surprised to see in the program a best woman alongside the best man, replacing the outmoded maid of honor. Next we were moved to see the bride and the groom come into the church with both parents on their arms, not merely the father. During the prayers of the faithful, the bride prayed for the grandparents who were dead. The couple recited their marriage vows in unison; then each presented the other with a ring, speaking the beautiful words of love and faithfulness which they so obviously understood and accepted. We truly witnessed them giving the sacrament to one another, uninterrupted by the usual promptings and repetitions of the priest. How strange that this sense of marriage as something chosen and witnessed directly by the people involved, engaging all of them in the couple's future, should be so seldom embodied in liturgical practice.

Although the stories and symbolism transmitted in our liturgy need continuing attention if they are to shape and strengthen us to become adult sharers of tradition, I am nevertheless constantly struck by its power to clarify the meaning of my life and renew my ties to the earth and all other people. For example, at a Benedictine priory that

I visit occasionally, great care is taken by the priest and the monks to stress the oneness of all who are present. The priest sits among us during the first part of the mass; different members of the congregation do the readings, which are echoed and amplified in the songs chosen by the choir—also sitting among the people—and repeated so that all can join in. No one tells anyone when to sit, stand or sing; it all takes place spontaneously and with unforced reverence. The spirit of relationship with the earth and each other that permeates this transformative celebration is expressed in the language of the hymn we sang once at communion:

> We are in
> the real presence
> We are the body of God
> We are the living and the dying
> Giving and receiving the bread of the Lord.

There is no higher and lower here, only different real people united in their humanity and their hope.

Such liturgy sends us back into the wider community to live in a renewed way. If we prefer an example of similar communication in a more down-to-earth setting, we can reread the conclusion of Dorothy Day's *The Long Loneliness:*

> We were just sitting there and people moved in on us. . . . I found myself, a barren woman, the joyful mother of children. . . . We cannot love God unless we love each other, and to love we must know each other. We know him in the breaking of bread, and we know each other in the breaking of bread, and we are not alone any

more. Heaven is a banquet and life is a banquet, too, even with a crust when there is companionship.

We have all known the long loneliness and we have learned that the only solution is to love and that love begins with community. It all happened when we sat there talking, and it is still going on.

9

A Mothering People?

The present moment is one of great threat and at the same time promise, depending on what kind of new order replaces the disorder of the Cold War. Many parts of the world are reverting to the restrictive identities of local nationalism, breeding antagonisms, while our own country is tempted to use its military power to ensure control of natural resources in poor countries. But more and more people are also aware, despite the turmoil and their lack of power, that they live on a small planet whose very life depends on how they use its limited resources, particularly its human resources. More than ever a concern for their development rather than their control seems essential. Whether the new order is to be forced from the top or created from the bottom will determine our future.

This agenda structures our identity and mission as church as well. John XXIII seems to have had an acute sense of these future possibilities. When he wrote *Peace on Earth* in 1963, he was trying to engage the church in the central struggle of humanity today. "What diversity in thy creatures, Lord! What wisdom has designed them all," he exclaimed, echoing the psalms. "The essential office of every public authority," he continued, should be "to safeguard the inviolable rights of the human person." He also insisted that it was the duty of every human person to work actively for solidarity, for:

Even though human beings differ from one another by virtue of their ethnic peculiarities, they all possess certain essential common elements, and are inclined by nature to meet each other in the world of spiritual values, whose progressive assimilation opens to them the possibility of perfection without limits. They have the right and duty therefore to live in communion with one another.

John insisted that working toward such communion was a personal obligation proceeding from "inner conviction," and that its foundation was not to be formed by equality of arms but by "mutual trust alone." He knew that the ability to have such trust depended on the willingness of people to do the hard work of rethinking tradition in new circumstances, of becoming fully human so they could be spiritual in the way the Spirit demanded today:

It is necessary that human beings, in the intimacy of their own consciences, should so live and act in their temporal lives as to create a synthesis between scientific, technical and professional elements on the one hand, and spiritual values on the other.

John's vision has the ring of truth, the power to evoke response, because it restores humanity to Christianity and Christianity to humanity. In calling the Second Vatican Council, he invited the whole church to respond to the same call. Many constructive changes were made after the council, but only now do we see that something more was being asked of the church: it was to become an enabler of people, so that all could participate as partners, and it would have to trust them when they did. Unfortunately, despite liturgical changes, the synods of bishops, and the development of priest councils, the church has not yet become such a trusting community; its divisions are more apparent than ever.

We now have different and conflicting notions of what the church is and should do, largely determined by whether we see it as offering a way of life or preserving a system of truth. Many resist the implications of the council, and continue to look at the church as the media do, as a powerful institution whose laws are established by the hierarchy from the top down, a kind of club that one should quit if the rules become onerous. But despite the excesses of church authority, such an understanding is a caricature of the way the church has actually operated in history. It also forgets that most rules are inevitably time-bound and need constant input from those for whom they are devised. The recent words of a thoughtful bishop show the predicament we are in. Commenting on the possibility of married priests serving in the face of the serious clergy shortage in the United States, he remarked that he would personally like to see the married priests return. "As a bishop I am still obedient to the Holy Father and the church's teaching. But humanly speaking, it looks like that is the way the church should go." If the church is to promote a way of life, it is this human base of the church that needs to be strengthened and integrated into the institution. And this can only be done by integrating the insights offered by the whole church through its people.

In theory, popes and bishops have frequently affirmed the principles of collegiality and subsidiarity, and they were echoed again at Vatican II. Dorothy Day gives a homespun description of subsidiarity in a previously unpublished article in *The Catholic Worker* of May 1988, applying it to any kind of government:

> The principle involved is the one stressed by the Popes. The State should not take over functions that can be performed by smaller bodies. It is like the mother doing everything herself in the house, on the grounds that she can do it better and easier and with less trouble. But how bad for the children's development and their sense of independence.

One reason the institutional church has had trouble turning over many functions to its people is because of motherly concern that her children will be confused. But if they are adults? There is still another difficulty. Part of the reason the church has had trouble accepting its full human identity is because it has excluded both women and the feminine values it wishes to preserve—caring, healing, helping others to grow—from its hierarchical organization and teaching office. Ironically, we have seen that if mothers are to act more successfully for themselves and others, they need to be strong, to think clearly, to relate to the wider community, and to plan for the years after their children are grown. As women today increasingly press for personal equality in public and private life, they are also challenging the church to rethink its traditional commitment to charity. It is a matter of uncovering the contemporary implications of St. Paul's insistence that no gifts, neither prophecy nor speaking in tongues, matter so much as the ability to incorporate love into our relationships with others. By defining itself in opposition to the feminine, western culture and the church have at their best tended to "help" women, but have not listened to their wisdom nor seen their strength. Women's testimony suggests that such charity should not be restricted to people's physical needs, but extended to the psychological, intellectual and spiritual aspects of their development. The deeper implication of Vatican II is that charity today means helping the people of God become the holding environment for human growth that good mothering provides. But this can be accomplished only by men and women who have restored mothering to their inner lives and outer work, who see themselves as sharers in the same process of growth.

The loving maternal face of the church has been so long obscured that every unexpected glimpse of it can astonish us. Today I see with fresh eyes the woman anointing Jesus with her perfume, the only one of his disciples present who understood the suffering and death he was about to undergo. When he tells us never to forget what she did, I know he means her compassion and understanding as well as her action, since one led to the other. I hear with new respect the voices of the three women leaving the tomb of Jesus, telling the apostles—who did not believe them—that it was empty. I admire the Samaritan woman at the well, able to listen to a stranger, capable of changing her life when he offers her hope that she can live as she truly wants, eager to share the news with her neighbors.

Of course, these are only fleeting reminders, far outnumbered by the endless photographs of massed clerics at official meetings, or television scenes of the pope's latest triumphal tour. But they remind me of other images: of Piero's Mary Magdalene, a guide holding a lantern, her other hand on her robe as if she is about to turn and we are to follow her light; of Julian of Norwich's beautiful image of the Trinity as Mother, our gracious God who covers us with the mantle of goodness. Julian also speaks of our

Mother Jesus holding the universe like a hazelnut in the palm of his hand, knowing "It lasts and always will because God loves it."

In a talk delivered at St. James Procathedral in Brooklyn in 1985, Carmelite sister Margaret Dorgan suggested that another way for all to open themselves to the feminine in God is by reaching to the contemplative depth within them. That depth requires a silencing of surface noise to reach "the listening quiet where God can speak. . . . Emerging from our contemplative depth, we look upon the ordinary world with new eyes. . . . At the very least, we'll be able to accept with good grace that others find the feminine in God." In addition, she now hears the words of Revelation, long applied to the church and to Mary, as a description of contemporary women's consciousness:

> Now a great sign appeared in heaven: a woman adorned with the sun, standing on the moon, and with the twelve stars on her head. She was pregnant and in labor, crying aloud in the pangs of childbirth.

But is it really possible for the church today to see and accept the feminine in God and itself? Even my retired pastor, whose sermons nourish the spirit, believes that the church as institution should be a well-disciplined army in order to survive. But armies today are changing as old walls are torn down and old enemies see themselves in a common struggle. Cooperation, negotiation, building a world economy, pose problems that cannot be solved by the use of force. Or perhaps we need to imagine a different kind of force, the kind native to mothering, not ruling or warring.

Searching for visual images for this new-old power in the church, I see a pregnant woman, a midwife, and a housewife. The vision of the first recalls the cover of this book. Angels pull back curtains to reveal the figure of a serious young woman announcing her pregnant condition to the world. Piero della Francesca painted this picture in the fifteenth century in honor of his own mother. It stands all alone, covered by a curtain the visitor must ask to have removed, in a tiny chapel in the cemetery where she is buried, on a hill overlooking her little village of Monterchi in northern Italy. As bearer of new life, this woman is eminently fit to represent the church of the gospel.

Amazingly, the figure the artist created is unsentimental and timeless, managing to unite physical, psychological and spiritual reality in its forthright portrayal of the holiness of childbearing. As one examines the figure more closely, its dissimilarity to most presentations of Mary, whether devotional or aesthetic, becomes more remarkable. She stands tall before us, deep in thought, yet aware of our presence. Her hand has unbuttoned the front of her blue gown for all to see the swelling white below, the proof of her pregnancy. The action of the angels places her center stage, saying that all honor in heaven and earth is given to this woman. She is not a queen, she is not receiving an angel's annunciation; she is making her own impressive annunciation to the world. She is Mary, she is Everymother, a reminder of the compassionate creator. She embodies a church with a different kind of strength than we see, for example, in the images of renaissance popes. Its power does not imply domination over others, but the ability to empower them because she is a vulnerable sharer among them.

This Mary is a human being, yet one who reveals instantly the presence of spirit in the processes of flesh. She reminds us that this presence is always possible, needing only our acknowledgement and attention. Her announcement is also a subtle appeal for the cooperation and welcome necessary to bring forth something new, in this case a child who is always about to come. The painting is a statement that birth and the life to follow it should be cause for public joy and public attention. They are not to be relegated to a hidden world of women culminating in what used to be called, so accurately, a "confinement."

This mother's proclamation of pregnancy makes us think about more than children, however. She heralds all potential new life: the human rebirth necessary for growth and fulfillment at any age. She asks for the food, shelter, education, friendship, consultation, and tolerance necessary to support it. New ideas as well as children must be helped to birth, even when they are as unexpected to hierarchies of power as were those of Jesus of Nazareth. This mother is the supreme symbol of that "holding" we have seen psychologists insist is necessary if people are to find and become themselves. She stands for every connection, every encounter that increases this process in body, mind or spirit. She appeals to creativity on every level and shows that it is based in community, not isolation. She is both protector and enabler, because she is human sharer.

Piero's painting makes me think of the way people provide similar "holding environments" for one another in daily life. I remember the stranger who carried my then ten year old son's dead collie home in his arms and stayed around for the burial. He had seen the dog leap in front of a car on the highway, had taken the trouble to park, read the tag around his neck, and find out where our house was. His kindness softened the terrible shock to my son. I think it helps explain why, some fifteen years later, he was able to ease his nineteen year old cat into a peaceful death. The two of them spent her last hours in a quiet communion. The ability to hold is passed on.

I too have felt the power of being held by strangers. Once, while bicycling on vacation, I suffered a sudden crash in a place where there was no one I knew. Bleeding and dazed, I was lifted up by men from a nearby firehouse. They would not accept my protestations that I was fine (which I was not) but dabbed the cuts on my face and insisted on having me checked out at the local hospital. They then returned me and the twisted bicycle to my temporary home. I will never forget the gentleness of those strong men.

The holding people do for one another can be psychological, of course, as well as physical. Although our oldest son died over twenty years ago, my husband told me just last week that if it had not been for the love he felt flowing from our friends, and their eloquent, healing words at the wake, the funeral and afterward, he would literally have fallen down. There are similar stories of being upheld in happier circumstances. I met a woman casually playing the piano on the last day of a biblical conference that was as warm in its reception of the people who came as in the excellence of its program. I recognized her as the organist at our concluding liturgy. After a few casual remarks about the sessions, this gray-haired woman turned to me and said, "I'm an Episcopalian, but I didn't miss a session. You see, I'm an orphan, too. The care I'm getting here among Catholic people is so upholding, I can't tell you how wonderful it feels."

The most intense holding environments, however, are those sustained by individuals with one another over long periods of time because they hold in tension both broken hopes and the possibility of reconciliation. Although it is usually interpreted as a parable of God's forgiveness of sinful humanity, the story of the prodigal son describes such a relationship. But as Jesus' prayer to his beloved Father shows, forgiving others is essential to that process of being forgiven.

Such reconciliation is a difficult achievement, much deeper than will, words or even behavior. Communication is its necessary threshold, but transformation of the self is required in order to take the risk of passing through the door after hurting and being hurt. When two who have been at odds begin to connect from the heart after separation and bitterness, however, the spirit they share is stronger than disappointment and even death.

Last fall two students told me different histories of reconciliations. The first came from a man in his forties who had left his native Caribbean home as a child of five, planting a tree before his departure so that if he ever returned he could see some physical sign that he belonged. At home his father was a respected doctor, but in the New York City neighborhood to which they moved—blue-collar, largely Irish Catholic—they were treated as ignorant immigrants, unable to speak the language.

As he grew, Carlos internalized their evaluation by feeling ashamed of his father and cutting himself off from his family. He dropped out of school and developed a serious drug habit. Even after he married (across ethnic lines) and held a regular job, he continued with drugs until a near-fatal accident led to an unexpected religious conversion.

At the time of the accident, as many times before, his father paid some immediate bills. But Carlos was confused and deeply embarrassed, still unable to build a relationship with someone he had hurt. Slowly the conversion gave him power to start mending his life. He began to get well acquainted with his two daughters, whom he had hardly known before, and forced himself to attend community college. There he took sociology, psychology and my course in African and Caribbean literature. He came to see a social context and cultural reasons for behavior he had thought was entirely his fault, and he decided to see his father again.

The last time he talked to me, Carlos and his family had just shared Thanksgiving dinner with his parents. His eyes shone, though he feels he is just taking his first steps to a new life. He had gone back once to his island birthplace to see the now towering tree he planted as a child. But he realizes that the trust and the love growing between father and son—the fruit of the father's patient love and Carlos' regained dignity—are the forces which make him belong in a world he now sees more realistically.

The other story, told me by a young woman who had been alienated from her mother for years, shows the power of mutual forgiveness after two people have hurt each other. As a daughter, Kathy told me, her mother disapproved of everything she did. That was part of the reason she was so wild at seventeen and had a baby she had to give up for adoption two years later. She has been married now for fifteen years, has three children and a good husband, but they have had hard times recently because of his poor health. At Christmas her mother visited. Kathy had not looked forward to it. But her mother had thought over the past; during the visit she looked at her daughter dispassionately and said: "You've had a very difficult life, haven't you?" And Kathy was able to agree. Her fears and resentments fell away; she talked to her mother as she had never before been able to. Their companionship—and the growing love between Kathy's children and their grandmother—is a new source of strength to her as she tries to meet the bills and work for the future.

Every day I see people providing holding environments like these for one another. I believe they are models of what we should be doing as church: helping to heal people, helping them to transform their lives by sharing our strengths and weaknesses.

Just as Piero's pregnant Mary symbolizes new life, a second feminine image of caring behavior, the midwife, represents the function of helping to bring such life into being. It is an apt image for the church we are looking for, because midwives cooperate with natural and social agents in specific contexts to help bring forth this life. Midwives believe in the emergence of spirit in and through flesh; they pay attention to the particular needs of the mother and the circumstances of her life. They encourage other family members, husband and children, to be present at the birth, to make it an occasion of celebration related to real, changing life commitments, rearranged to welcome the unknown, powerless stranger entering the family.

Like the Mexican-American woman in the last chapter, who made a statue of a pregnant Mary, midwives celebrate sex and pregnancy as the root of all life. They do not see sex in terms of temptation or duty, but as an intimate form of communication, passionate and physical, combining pleasure and creativity. Unlike the negative attitudes found in so many manuals of moral theology, this view harmonizes with the biblical understanding of sexual union as "knowing" and with its frequent use in mystical literature as an image of union with God.

Midwives would no doubt prefer to bring forth the child of someone like the mother in Piero's painting, who has obviously chosen to bring it into the world. Close to the web of life surrounding real pregnancy, they could not treat conception simply as an act of "nature" or insist that women have as many children as possible. They know that the mothers and fathers they aid would be abdicating both consciousness and conscience if they did not plan intelligently as well as generously for those children they could hope to raise well. Midwives must deal with real duties and abilities, not theoretical ones, for God has placed them in real circumstances. Midwives would consider it a duty to help women plan their families, introducing them to the safest, least harmful kinds of contraception so they would have some choice.

As for abortions, a midwife would be all too aware of how different public and ecclesial standards are for other acts of violence—war, for instance, in which all kinds of circumstances are taken into consideration when judging the moral guilt involved. In general, she would prefer not to assist with abortions, although she would empathize with the woman who feels she cannot go through with a particular pregnancy. She could never be as certain as churchmen that every conception should be brought to term, preferring the example of Jesus, who told those who threw stones at the woman taken in adultery to go home and reflect on their own sins. A midwife would uphold traditional ideals and insist that a woman recognize the element of violence in any abortion, but she would support the woman, whatever her decision. The midwife would recognize that there is almost never a purely virtuous or purely evil act; her concern would be that the woman's decision be as conscientious as possible, and that it not be based on fear or pressure from others.

I hardly needed convincing that having an abortion is always a matter for grief; my student Kathy made me aware that sometimes not having an abortion can be just as painful a decision, with equally serious moral implications.

When she was nineteen, she felt it would be wrong to abort her child, so she gave birth to a baby daughter and put her up for adoption. In those days, she was not allowed to learn anything about the people who adopted her. When the Lisa Steinberg story hit the papers a few years ago with lurid details of inhuman cruelty to an adopted child, Kathy began to have nightmares. She realized that her own daughter might have been mistreated or killed and she would have done nothing to prevent it. Worst of all, she would never know for sure.

Seeing how our society dehumanizes and objectifies sex, the church as midwife would examine her own conscience. She would acknowledge that she had denigrated both sex and women, in the process disfiguring the image of the creator as well. While continuing to honor a life of freely chosen celibacy, her teaching would reflect the centrality of sex in human life; after consulting married people and other mature members of the community, she would reformulate her guidance for young people to try to help them deal humanly and morally with their sexuality —no easy task at best, but a positive, supportive attitude would help.

A midwife church would realize that working for the true equality of the sexes in power and decision-making roles is an essential ingredient in reestablishing the human, social, and sacred context of sexual relations. She would confess that Pope Paul VI's decision, however idealistic, to dismiss the church's highly qualified international commission on birth control because they came to conclusions that contradicted then-current official teaching was a terrible mistake, contributing in practice to the growing acceptance of abortion. More positively, the church as midwife would reinforce women's self-esteem and develop their power of decision-making from the time they were born.

Because those who admired the methods of Socrates in drawing forth from people what they did not know they knew called him a midwife, the term has long been used as an image for educators who bring new ideas to life. As educator, the midwife-church would concentrate not only on bringing new physical lives into the world, but on enabling them to participate fully in public life and in community with one another. She would encourage massive grassroots political involvement among the faithful. After all, unless the communities in which babies grow up and become adults are transformed, providing protection for an endangered planet, good education, housing, and human work, the infants whose chance for existence she champions can never enjoy the blessings the creator intends for them.

Such a midwife-educator would come to see that focusing on the prevention of abortion as clear evil is sometimes a self-serving action on the part of those who do not have to make the difficult decisions. As novelist Margaret Atwood has so imaginatively suggested in *The Handmaid's Tale*, authoritarian attempts to control women and childbearing are not only doomed to defeat, but they may also reveal the often unconscious hypocrisy of those who try to enforce them. Only when the church is a vulnerable sharer like the pregnant woman or the midwife can she assist and encourage new life and decisions to emerge even from poor and sinful beginnings, the very places in which Jesus most frequently exercised his ministry.

A teacher as midwife is always concerned for the possibility of new thought emerging to vitalize the old. She knows that truth is not kept alive in ecclesiastical decrees but in human minds. The midwife-church would care more for thinking than for thought, as philosopher Hannah Arendt did, valuing genuine personal response more than memorized repetition or agreement. She would also agree with Arendt—though few of the philosopher's male colleagues then did—that the exercise of heavy-handed power revealed an absence of true power. Arendt was thinking first of all of military power; in the church we might apply her reflection to the silencing of theologians and threats of excommunication against independent lay people. The power of a mother church, instead of trying to shut out or destroy those who disagree, would spend itself in emphasizing what its members hold in common and be tireless in its efforts at reconciliation.

But how can the church fulfill its institutional responsibilities without stressing beaureaucratic organization or resorting to force? I would suggest a third feminine image, that of the housewife. In a playful mood I once even pointed out similarities between the roles of pope and housewife:

> The temptations for popes and housewives are much the same, it seems. Keeping things from rust and the moth is a full-time job, and someone has to be responsible. Deterioration sets in, then hopelessness follows and human morale is lowered.
>
> In the more complicated webs of human relations, however, mothers and popes seem to have even more in common. Both exist to nourish and nurture their children; both aim at fostering that combination of vision and responsibility in

their charges that will enable them to become adults who will not need such care, and may be able to give it to others.

But being constantly inside one place, whether it is home or the Vatican, also tends to make the occupant more aware of all the inside work that needs doing rather than of the needs of those in the wide world outside. One who has peeled with the paint, suffered with the rot and mildew, and grown furious with clutter knows very well how such struggles can stretch out and make one lose a sense of proportion about people's feelings and world events.

Today I offer the housewife as model for the church a little more seriously. It is a lowly role that has been largely occupied by women, and has been so denigrated that women themselves seek other terms like "homemaker" or prefer to list their part-time jobs when they have to describe themselves in public documents. Though taking care of a home and its inhabitants is a constructive and significant role, it takes a leap of the imagination for many men or women to see the image of the housewife as a positive one. Yet the job is really that of an economist, a manager. Unlike a bureaucrat who thinks exclusively in terms of the products and profits of his company, a good economist today must work toward a more human community.

Bureaucrats are not bad people—many are competent and well intentioned—but because their responsibility is always clearly limited, by definition they are not working for the common welfare. The good housewife, on the other hand, though hardly powerful politically, cannot divide her obligations. She is responsible for keeping the home in order for the use and convenience of others, a job that requires breadth of mind, social skills and basic generosity as well as efficiency. She must keep on good terms with the neighbors as well as those who provide the goods and services she needs in order to care for her own household. She has to have a good idea of what's going on not only in the neighborhood but also in the economy as a whole.

One of her chief obligations is her responsibility for providing and preparing food for all to share. In the traditional European home, where the family returned home for lunch, the housewife controlled their nourishment as few American women can today. When Virginia Woolf portrayed Mrs. Ramsay, an image of the ideal traditional woman, in *To the Lighthouse*, she placed her accurately at the head of a dinner table, providing warmth and nourishment to body and spirit through her boeuf en daube and her skillful orchestration of the conversational strengths of those around her. Even in her everyday life the good housewife knows what to keep on the shelf or in the refrigerator (rice, a good pasta, a red onion, peppers or mushrooms, some garlic and other spices, olive oil, cheese and fresh fruit) so that with or without a little fish or leftover meat, she can serve any unexpected guest a palatable meal without fuss.

Food has always been central to religion as it is to human life. Celebrations in honor of all gods involve elaborate meals, though often they also require the sacrifice of animals as burnt offerings. Jesus instituted the sacrament of the eucharist at the last Passover supper he shared with his followers before he died. During that meal he offered himself as food and drink for all future generations, whenever his followers would eat together in memory of him.

Unfortunately, we tend to forget that eucharist means

thanksgiving and ignore its connection with real food; remembering would give us a deeper sense of the action in which we were participating. Food is a natural symbol of sacrifice; one form of life eats another all the way up the food chain. In meals, the work of those who have gathered and cooked it is mingled in offering with the food. The effort that goes into preparing a dinner party is not for sale or profit, but for the consumption, enjoyment and sharing that marks true friendship. At a deeper level, the eucharist should infuse the life experience of those who share it with powerful symbolic meaning. What a difference it would make if we retained an interior awareness of its reality when we share a bounteous Thanksgiving meal with family and friends!

Not long ago, I came across an old cheesecake recipe of my mother—dead forty years now—and felt I had to try it. Following the slightly fading advice she had penned on one side of a 3 × 5 card, I was able to recreate a cake which tasted exactly as I remember it from age ten. As with Proust's madelaine, its first taste flooded my memory with people and times long since disappeared. I began to understand the exclamation of the psalmist: "O taste and see that the Lord is sweet." It helped me see more clearly how the preparation and serving of ordinary food could be a holy service, capable of building a loving community and handing down tradition through the generations, connecting the living and the dead. Dorothy Day meant something quite profound when she insisted that the only authority at the Catholic Worker was the cook; nourishing people with food for body and spirit is surely the central task of the church.

A good housewife is also a good worker, attentive to both the task and the people involved. This aspect of the role challenges us in all kinds of jobs. Good editors, for instance, pay careful attention to works written by others, helping them to sharpen and extend their ideas, taking trouble to help them find the best words and structure in which to express them. Last summer I walked by a house from which I heard music playing and discovered that six or seven men were working together behind it. They were clearly familiar with their tools and each other, laughing and talking while they worked. When I got closer, I saw that they were building a deck on the back of the house. I smiled, realizing that they too were providing a holding environment, one in which people could sit and talk as they looked at the swans and the stars.

There are many unexpected kinds of cooperative, useful work. It need not be paid in money; housewives seldom are, though we ought to find appropriate ways in which to reward the help they give neighbors as well as family members. Sometimes in their spontaneous responses they may not even realize how they are serving others. A spunky nun in her late seventies recently confided, "I had a humiliating experience last month. I am slowly losing my eyesight and my doctor sent me to the optometrist to see if something could be done before I had to have a cataract operation. I'm working on the history of our order, you know. I'm familiar with our French past as well as our present international communities, and I want to pass on our story for all our sisters. And I'm still a trustee of the hospital, where I help make some decisions that matter. When this man saw me, he was so sure of himself. 'I see no point in doing anything for someone so old. Just go home,' he said straight off. I can't tell you how small I felt; there seemed nothing left. But when I got home, I began to think. It's wrong for him to make old people feel this way—that they are useless. And I went on thinking: it is not just me he hurt. It is the poor I help as well." So she went back to the optometrist, gathering up her words and her spirit, and told him he should not tell old people that they have no future, that there is no point in helping them see. This time he took the trouble to examine her.

In the economy of salvation, this nun was a good housewife. And ultimately, the function of the housewife-church should be such sound economic management. To be effective, however, it must be the kind of management that the philosopher-economist E.F. Schumacher envisaged, one that sees the brains and souls of human beings as central resources, utilizes them, and does not waste them. In his book *Good Work*, Schumacher sees most of our business and governmental institutions managing from the top down, something he calls the Christmas tree model, pointed at the top, heavy at the bottom where no initiative is encouraged. In practice, this style leads to a tremendous waste of resources and is ultimately inefficient. The style that works calls for minimal administration from the top; the model here is of someone holding a bunch of balloons in her hand on different strings, each one with its own initiative and control.

Schumacher makes some excellent practical suggestions as to how to move gradually from one style of management to the other. He recommends the "lifeboat" approach, transforming at least one small sector of the economy so we know how to survive if the rest collapses. The method, which rests on understanding society and developing relationships within it, is to tap in to what already exists in society, not to try to duplicate it. Schumacher suggests linking up with different networks to find out and get what you need. Carrying out an overall integrated plan will require thinkers, doers, and communicators. He advises delegating authority for the separate processes involved in making and distributing the product. The first requirement, of course, is that you produce something people really need, and not stimulate an artificial need for something you can make profitably. Naturally, this implies that people are consulted, that a real study has been made of community needs. Management of this sort would enable workers to respect themselves and their work as they should.

Schumacher describes three traditional functions of work: to help people use and develop their faculties, to help people overcome ego by joining with others in common tasks, and to bring forth goods and services that we all need. Obviously, the first step toward reeducation for this approach to work is to think differently about human beings and the purpose of life.

It seems that human needs coincide today, whatever perspective we adopt. There is a striking parallel between the good management Schumacher suggests for any viable economic enterprise and the kind that would be suitable and effective in the church. And such management exists for the same reasons, to provide the opportunity for the people it affects to become more conscious, freer, more creative as they consider how to make the best use of the earth's resources.

Pregnant woman, midwife, housewife: these feminine images and symbols represent the human virtues and qualities people in the church need to value and develop if the church is to build a community capable of passing on a living tradition, responding creatively to a constantly evolving world. In this process, it should not neglect a largely untapped pool of human resources: our wise old men and women. Erik Erikson's final revision of his life cycle theory states that this last stage of life sums up and contains all the virtues of the others; we can benefit from the wisdom our old ones have gained through a lifetime of experience.

Last spring a friend of mine was inspired to ask our pastor to celebrate a special Sunday mass in honor of parishioners who are over eighty, to show them we appreciated them while they could still get to church. The pastor was cooperative, volunteers interviewed our fifteen delighted octogenarians, and their lively, sometimes unexpected opinions were printed in a newsletter handed out at the mass. The woman who suggested the celebration was permitted to speak at the mass, which delighted the congregation; the whole service communicated a sense of vitality, reverence, and quiet good humor.

In recent years I have interviewed dozens of men and women in their seventies and eighties. They are largely humble, cheerful folk whose circle of interest and affection extends to ever-widening groups of humanity. Their personal networks cross and replenish our public life, yet they are often the "Invisibles" there. The nun whose eyes were going bad but insisted the doctor should do something spoke up not just for herself but also for other old people who might not have her courage or her resources.

I think of Mildred, my eighty-nine year old ex-student and long-time friend; she calls *me* teacher, but in fact our relationship is the reverse. She was one of the first women elders in her Presbyterian church and a member of the choir until last year. Still living in the house her grandfather built and in which she grew up, she has great-grandchildren who range from ministers to fundamentalist Moslems, all of whom revere her. She calls her Moslem son-in-law the best Christian she knows, but she resists her Moslem grandchildren's repeated attempts to convert her. Loving all her relatives and her wide circle of friends, she has widened her knowledge of other religions and people through several visits to the Near East.

Mildred has not had an easy life, bringing up her three children alone, with slim financial resources. After surviving several serious heart attacks, she is living with the doctor's warning in her ears: "If you go home without a triple bypass, you're liable to die any day just going up the stairs."

It's been almost two years since he made that remark. Mildred does not feel well; an ex-librarian and a great reader, she asks "Why does God keep me here in my epilogue?" but she keeps on going. As she has for decades, she continues to write verses of high quality and good humor to newborn babies, sick friends, and local celebrities, and her letters to politicians, columnists and dead poets reveal her deep personal commitment to justice. Like the pictures on her wall, from the cartoon animals of great-grandchildren to the portraits of relatives, friends, and presidents, Mildred lives and connects because she continues to share herself with those she encounters.

Men, of course, also have wisdom to share. Having been refused ordination as a priest with no reason given after years of study in an Irish monastery, Gary McEoin, now eighty-two, has made positive use of an experience that might have caused others to leave the church. Instead, he became a lawyer, an historian and a linguist, supporting himself as a journalist with a special expertise on Latin America. His more than twenty-five books have introduced thousands to the meaning of Vatican II, liberation theology, the complexities of Northern Ireland, and U.S. responsibility for continuing exploitation in Central America, but he has never had a best-seller and is primarily concerned to enable others to continue his work for justice. Living on next to nothing but the friendship of those who enjoy his presence, he quietly continues to aid a Salvadoran refugee stopped at the border by our distorted immigration policies, share his wealth of information and contacts with a young woman setting off to Latin America for the first time, and listen to the anxieties of those he has just met. A grieving widower, his is a stripped-down life, in which he is always prepared to set off again, most of his earthly possessions in a backpack, ready to do a job of writing, share his laughter and his stories, clear-sighted but never bitter about the tasks ahead.

Mildred and Gary represent just two of the extraordinary resources among us that we as people of the church should tap. Other older people may need a ride, or physical care, but they are also worth hearing, and consulting at every level. In the terms of this book, they may need mothering, but they can mother us even more, nourish, enable and share with us, enriching us in ways beyond our imagining. Despite the needed revolution against the gerontocracy that controlled the curia at the end of Vatican II, I would place old people in advisory positions, for limited terms, at every level of church administration. Peopling Vatican offices with international cadres of grandparents, great-aunts and great-uncles may be one of our best hopes for revitalizing tradition.

But can a church, divided as we know it to be, transform itself into such a mothering community? Certainly, we can begin to do it as individuals, no matter who or where we are. The project is realistic only for long-distance runners, who realize that there will never be a time when they will not need to grow, and who also recognize without bitterness that they will probably not live to see their hopes for the church fulfilled. The important thing is: keep on running—or walking if you are like me.

The question, of course, is not simply a matter of individual action: Can we as a church take a journey toward transformation together even though we start from such different places? Many groups as well as individuals already are on such journeys—independent prayer groups, base communities, organizations of married priests who wish to serve again in the active ministry, volunteers meeting urban or rural needs and living in community, hundreds serving in hospices or working with those suffering with AIDS, dedicated teachers in inner-city schools. The images and resources I have affirmed are partly a reflection of the new power and authority emerging in unexpected places. But Walt Kelly's Pogo was telling the truth about the church when he said that we had met the enemy and he is us. We are still divided, from each other and often within ourselves. We live in this tension, and I hope the process of reeducation I have shared in this book should help others realize that we must accept it. We all need to learn better how to live lovingly with others who disagree with us, who hold different ideas because of different experiences.

Those of us who believe that perception is a product of our development, of course, differ in particular from those who see ideas as essences, as things. But we should never forget that all differences, even this one, reside in people who are to be cherished. We should not hire public relations experts to manipulate people to accept views they do not hold. It is no pious evasion of personal effort to remind ourselves that it is the Spirit who will accomplish the needed work in the church; it is still our responsibility to elicit the deepest identities in ourselves and others through listening, loving attention, and care. We cannot grow toward community by insisting that we are right but only by learning to share our stories.

Willa Cather has given us one model of such a community in her portrayal of the church in *Death Comes for the Archbishop.* In this novel the rose and gold of the sky over Rome in the Prologue, when the cardinals pick French missionary priest Jean La Tour to be the first archbishop of Santa Fe, are later reflected in the gold and rose of the rocks in the ragged, unformed New Mexican landscape he chooses to make into his cathedral. The rock of Rome is mirrored in the high rock of Acoma where the Indians celebrate mass. His judgment is slow against personal and cultural aberrations as he tries to plant an old tradition in a new world. Authority here consults Indians, scouts, women, and often abides by their advice. Accompanying the old bondservant Sada to church one night, the archbishop realizes that "this church was Sada's house, and he was a servant in it."

The archbishop learns to live with growing respect for the differences of others, in particular his energetic and decidedly less ascetic vicar, Fr. Vaillant. Fr. La Tour is quite open to the unity of physicality and spirit: "Time and again the Bishop had seen a good dinner, a bottle of claret, transformed into spiritual energy under his very eyes." He is equally tolerant and loving of the different theological interpretations of his trusted friend, though he gently disagrees with his vicar's statement that people need miracle:

> The miracles of the church seem to me to rest not so much upon faces or voices or healing power coming suddenly near to us from afar off, but upon our perceptions being made finer, so that for a moment our eyes can see and our ears can hear what is there about us always.

He talks with Indians just as he does to his superiors in Rome, and the young guide Jacinto sees no false face on the bishop as he has on most white people. Jacinto thought this remarkable and it enables him both to talk to the priest and to save his life by giving him shelter in a sacred cave he would not have felt free to show to any other white man. Though clearly this archbishop is a nineteenth century Frenchman in New Mexico, his understanding of the church is a model for us as well. Having learned to grow in every encounter with others as he remains faithful to his God and the church, he is also able to face death as another life passage, a journey at one with those he has already made. He is a strong man in a strong maternal church of adults. Cather's vision of the church is wholly sacramental.

One final image presents another model. It is the picture of Chaucer's pilgrims on their way to Canterbury in another period of great social and economic upheaval marking the beginning of the modern world. They too are different in every way: in class, sex, age, education, moral worth, and attitudes to the church itself. But there they are, on the road together, telling each other their stories, staying overnight and eating at the same inn. It would be a great example to follow today when we are at the breakup of a world of competing nuclear superpowers and on the edge of a possible human society. As we come to share the common story of the earth as our mother, we can all speak and listen, learning to love the differences among its people and traditions. On this pilgrimage through space and time, we can still learn to respond to the Spirit so that we too may renew the earth.

10

Message from Old Mother Church

I warned you earlier that an old, old woman had become so real in my mind that I knew she was going to take over my book. Maybe it's been hers from the beginning, but now she's here in my living room. She's sitting down in the rocking chair.

Old Mother Church rocks back and forth, her eyes closed. She seems lost in her memories, but she's starting to talk softly. "If my children are to learn the way of love, they do not need to turn to theologians for answers but rather to become theologians of their lives. They must give themselves up to that constant action of sharing that makes us free. It is creation—perhaps that is why it is so hard for them to let go and mother one another.

"Ah, but this mothering is a long, painful process," old Mother Church groans. "I know Christ is always with me, but there are times when it's hard to recognize his presence. Sometimes I feel as if I'm only an earthly mother, caring, but all too powerless." Now she looks at me directly. "But I have made a decision. My children must learn to swim in the seas of humankind if they are to fulfill the promise of their baptism. They will have to do it themselves."

She's rising from the chair now and handing me a long

sheet of paper. "I'm going away for a while. This will tell you why, and how to get in touch." She starts to walk out the door, and turns back. "I want you to give them my message," she says, "it's everything I've learned."

"O my children, how long it has been since I talked to you all together. How my heart weeps when I think of how you have become so divided. I remember the many times and ways I failed you and even let your differences turn into conflict. Believe me, I did not do it intentionally, but out of ignorance and my desire to be the best mother I could. I wanted to show that I was the one who loved you most; I wanted heaven and earth for you, but ended up restricting you and perhaps hurting you as much as I helped. I know it now. I didn't then.

"I wanted to do more for you than my older sister Nature had. She kept telling me how long she had struggled to bring you forth, how exhausting it was, and how boring life was before you could talk to her. She longed for your conversation and my companionship, but I was suspicious of her earthy ways, her sensuality, the way she reveled even in violent storms, earthquakes, volcanoes, and strange, underwater beasts. Now I realize that I overprotected you, insisting that you separate yourself from all those playful children of hers in the wind and the trees. I thought I was showing reverence for the Spirit, but I was really jealous of her spirits, and I realize now that I overdid it. I cut you off from your natural mother in my eagerness to show you that she was not your true creator. Unintentionally, I cramped your development just at the time you were beginning to grow in numbers and influence. And how could I have allowed you to come to see the Jews as enemies, and begin the tragic history of teaching contempt for the Lord's own people?

"Then—how ashamed I am now to think of it—I began to value Roman power more than I did the example of Mary and Peter; they had been humble but remained strong in siding with all of you, not with money or the authorities. When I decided to support Constantine in battle, I gave you a terrible example which you have followed all too faithfully. His mother Helen knew it and tried to set me straight, but I was intoxicated with the sign of the cross on military banners, coming at the head of all those dashing soldiers on horseback.

"It became second nature for you to think you should fight, though next it would be against the children of your older brother Ishmael. For centuries you killed and were killed in my name, defending my honor, and I never disabused you. I loved the color and thrill of chivalry—I was still young, but old enough to be vain.

"Some saints, like Clare and Francis, and some artists, like Piero, knew even then that giving life, sustaining and appreciating it, were far more important than winning battles. Less exciting for the winners, but so much more constructive for everyone else, particularly women and children. They remembered that the cross stood for a different kind of conflict. But I sometimes forgot.

"Oh, I have much to repent. I encouraged you, my children, to stamp out the joy of paganism, my older sister's religion. I let you destroy the reverence for the life of the grain, the juice of the grape, the courtesy of mutual sacrifice in the vegetable and animal worlds. I wanted you to forget that the great shrines you built to God were built over those to the Great Mother Goddess whom I despised. But when you came to understand God only as a Father, chiefly as a patriarchal ruler, you lost contact with the earth and the living things that were an essential part of

God's great goodness. I did not trust enough in that goodness. I wanted to be your only mother.

"Yes, like any earthly woman, I thought I had to be the only influence on my children. I see now that I often confused my own ideas and hopes with those of God. If only I had known then what I know now! How much better it would have been for you and the earth if I had encouraged you to accept different influences, to merge the new with the old, as you did so well with Christmas and Easter symbols. Instead, I cut my family off from other groups, separated them so severely that we lost our sense of relatedness and many of our riches. For centuries I did not speak up—at least not loudly enough—when you were enslaving other members of the family, violating all the mandates we had been given. To think that my family used words like infidel, heretic, schismatic, witch, and I encouraged them! Christians even vilified and executed other Christians in my name. Those who revolted against me, whom I should still have considered my children, carried these destructive practices over to the New World; countries that thought themselves Christian dominated and exploited peoples they considered backward. How grateful I am that we have begun to see the world as one, that the God of history and science has led nations to change their ways and given me a chance to reflect and change mine, to become the kind of mother that the creator who loves the earth and all its creatures really wants.

"Before I learned all this, however, even in the twentieth century, my narrowness and inattention made me an accomplice in the sacrilegious destruction of millions of God's first people. Nothing is possible now but atonement and penance and the firm decision never again to look on any people as outsiders.

"Mea culpa! Mea culpa! I must look honestly at my

failures in history and accept my heavy responsibility for what they have produced. But I must stop there and not lay it on my children. Mothers are all too apt to give their children too great a sense of guilt, but it only blocks the growth of conscience and the possibility of fresh thinking on their part.

"Well, I have tried to make amends. Previously, I was teaching according to the way I understood things—much of it was wrong, and I did not convey the rest clearly enough. But surely you realize that I always wanted you to do what our loving creator wanted. Now, as old ideologies and powers are beginning to crumble, you have a new opportunity to do so. You have a new chance to be co-creators of that peaceful kingdom Jesus came to announce. But remember, you are a pregnant people; you must labor to bring forth not only the children, but the ideas and the stories that can make the old vision live today. With the help of the Spirit, you must complete the work of the Incarnation.

"On this fragile, shimmering earth parents and teachers have always told stories to children so that they can know their ancestors in all their wisdom and foolishness. Spider and tortoise tales have moved from Africa to the Caribbean and to the southern states, affirming the survival qualities of ingenious and creative people in a dangerous universe, or one in which they were dominated and despised by those in power over them.

"My people too have told my story in different ways in different cultures. Jesus was Jewish and spoke Aramaic, of course, but Paul wrote in Greek. My saints and artists have been Asian, European, Latin American, African, male and female. The Virgin of Guadalupe spoke in Indian, wearing the blue-green Aztec royal color. Children in every culture should learn that the eternal God longs for their unique existence, their qualities essential to the weaving of the world. Never be afraid in the darkness of night or when you are alone under the starry sky, because your ancestors assure you that the maker of that sky is as concerned for each of you as for the universe.

"When you realize this, you will not be afraid to stand up freely and begin to tell your own stories. It will take energy to follow them to the end, to shape them in as many different structures as possible, mirroring the endless variety of creation. Pain and joy will thread through them, for every story must have tension and conflict, yet God's imagination is infinite, and my daughter Julian has assured us that 'all manner of things shall be well.'

"The adventure lies ahead of you, yet it is my adventure, too. Through your stories I will be continuing to tell the good news in fresh ways. My people will no longer spend their time arguing about the meaning of the texts; they will dramatize the meaning in their lives. A growing network of people will interpret the religious story anew, knowing that it is also part of the new story of science: the one that does not dominate the earth but listens to it and interprets its story. This new Genesis stresses the constancy of change and adaptation necessary to preserve life; it reveals how people of different races and colors have always adapted successfully to changing climates and circumstances.

"For those who accept the findings of this story, tribal and racial stereotypes will disappear. A fascinating variety will be seen to mark the evolution of life, each form transcending itself within a higher, more unified form of life. It will no longer be a matter of dominating and exploiting the earth, but of appreciating its marvels and using them wisely. This new story of science enables my people to know that they are one family on a tiny, traveling planet.

Yet God's story ennobles even this story, reassuring its hearers as a mother does her child at bedtime, that they can trust in the maker of this living creation.

"Do not be afraid, my children, when I tell you that I have decided to retire. Yes, I intend to rejoin my older sister Nature once again. After all these eons we are becoming reconciled. So do not be discouraged about the quarrels you have not yet resolved. You are grown up now; you have the means to settle them if you want. Listen, talk, find common ground. Remember that our concern should always be for the poor and powerless, whom earthly powers will still wish to ignore. I beg of you to learn from my failures that the use of force is really the absence of true understanding and right persuasion. It reveals the inability to engage in face-to-face meetings, to deal with difference in other ways than by trying to destroy it. The time has come for you to face each other with no weapons except those of the spirit.

"I'm not leaving you altogether, of course. But I'm taking my own advice and giving up control. I waited almost too long. But don't worry; I'll still be a member of the family who comes to dinner whenever you ask me, eager to hear the news and to tell you what I think. Believe me, you can carry on. I have over-protected you and stifled your initiative. No more. Stretch your minds and hearts and extend your hands to one another; there has been too much destruction of body and mind. A pregnant people should nurture one another.

"Remember, I love you and I trust you. Goodbye; the future is in your hands."

Works Cited

Adams, Henry. "The Dynamo and the Virgin." *The Education of Henry Adams.* New York: Random House, 1931.

———. *Mont Saint Michel and Chartres.* Princeton: Princeton University Press, 1981.

Allman, John. "Motherless Creation: Motifs in Science Fiction." *North Dakota Quarterly* 58, no. 2, Spring 1990, 124–132.

Atwood, Margaret. *Surfacing.* New York: Warner Books, 1983.

———. *The Handmaid's Tale.* New York: Random House, 1985.

Barciauskas, Rosemary Curran, and Debra Beery Hull. *Loving and Working: Reweaving Women's Public and Private Lives.* New York: Meyer-Stone Books, 1989.

Bateson, Mary Catherine. "Caring for Children, Caring for the Earth." *Christianity and Crisis* 31, March 1980, 67–70.

Belenky, Mary Field, Blythe McVicken Clinchy, Nancy Rule Goldberger, and Jill Mattuch Terule. *Women's Ways of Knowing.* New York: Basic Books, 1986.

Bel Geddes, Joan. "Charity Really Does Begin at Home— with Oneself." *Holiness and Mental Health.* Mahwah, Paulist Press, 1972.

Berry, Thomas. "Wonderworld, Wasteworld and the Earth." *Cross Currents* XXXV, no. 4, Winter 1985– 86, 408–422.

Boulding, Elise. "The Vision Is the Reality." *Cross Currents* XXX, no. 4, Winter 1980–1981, 441–453.

Bynum, Caroline Walker. *Jesus as Mother: Studies in the Spirituality of the High Middle Ages.* Berkeley: University of California Press, 1984.

Cunneen, Sally. *A Contemporary Meditation on the Everyday God.* Chicago: Thomas More Press, 1976.

———. *Sex: Female; Religion: Catholic.* New York: Holt, Rinehart and Winston, 1968.

Erikson, Erik. *Identity and the Life Cycle.* New York: W. W. Norton, 1980.

Gilligan, Carol. "Woman's Place in Man's Life Cycle." *In a Different Voice: Psychological Theory and Women's Development.* Cambridge: Harvard University Press, 1982, 5–23.

Gordon, Mary. *The Company of Women.* New York: Ballantine Books.

Hebblethwaite, Margaret. *Motherhood and God.* London: Geoffrey Chapman, 1984.

The Homeric Hymns. Trans. Charles Boer. Chicago: The Swallow Press, 1970.

John XXIII. *Peace on Earth.* Vatican Polyglot Press, 1963.

Kegan, Robert. *The Evolving Self: Problem and Process in Human Development.* Cambridge: Harvard University Press, 1982.

Keller, Evelyn Fox. *Reflections on Gender and Science.* New Haven: Yale University Press, 1985.

Kitzinger, Sheila. *Women as Mothers.* New York: Random House, 1978.

Klinger, Kurt. *A Pope Laughs: Stories of John XXIII.* Trans. Sally Cunneen. New York: Holt, Rinehart and Winston, 1964.

Kolbenschlag, Madonna. *Lost in the Land of Oz: The Search for Identity and Community in American Life.* San Francisco: Harper & Row, 1988.

L'Engle, Madeleine. "The Possible Human." *Cross Currents* XXXVIII, no. 4, Winter 1988–89, 385–394.

Lightfoot, Sara. *Balm in Gilead: Journey of a Healer.* New York: Addison-Wesley, 1988.

Malangatana, Valente. "Woman." *The Penguin Book of Modern African Poetry.* Gerald Moore and Ulli Beier, eds. New York: Penguin Books, 1984.

Martin, Emily. *The Woman in the Body: A Cultural Analysis of Reproduction.* Boston: Beacon Press, 1987.

Maxwell-Smith, Florida. *The Measure of My Days.* New York: Penguin Books, 1979.

Merchant, Carolyn. *The Death of Nature: Women, Ecology and the Scientific Revolution.* San Francisco: Harper & Row, 1980.

Merton, Thomas. *Eighteen Poems.* New York: New Directions, 1985.

Milhaven, Annie Lally. *The Inside Stories.* Mystic: Twenty-Third Publications, 1987.

Milhaven, J. Giles. "A Medieval Lesson on Bodily Knowing: Women's Experience and Men's Thought." *Journal of the American Academy of Religion* LVII, no. 2, 341–371.

Moore, Sebastian. "Jesus the Liberation of Desire." *Cross Currents* XL, no. 4, Winter 1990–91.

"Mother Church." *The New Catholic Encyclopedia.* New York: McGraw-Hill, 1967.

Murdoch, Iris. *The Sovereignty of Good.* New York: Schocken Press, 1971.

Neumann, Erich. *The Great Mother: An Analysis of the Archetype.* Trans. Ralph Manheim. Bollingen Series: Princeton University Press, 1972.

Noddings, Nel. *Caring.* Berkeley: University of California Press, 1984.

O'Brien, Mary. *The Politics of Reproduction.* Boston: Routledge, Kegan Paul, 1981.

Ochs, Carol. *Women and Spirituality.* Totowa: Rowman and Allanheld, 1983.

O'Connor, Flannery. "A Temple of the Holy Ghost." *The Complete Stories.* New York: Farrar, Straus and Giroux, 1976.

Olsen, Tillie. "I Stand Here Ironing." *Tell Me a Riddle.* New York: Delacorte Press, 1956.

―――. *Silences.* New York: Delacorte Press, 1978.

―――. *Yonnondio From the Thirties.* New York: Dell Publishing Co., Inc., 1975.

Rasmussen, Larry. "Reinhold Niebuhr: Public Theologian." *Cross Currents* XXXVIII, no. 2, Summer 1988, 198–218.

Raymo, Chet. *Honey from Stone: A Naturalist's Search for God.* New York: Penguin Books, 1989.

Rich, Adrienne. *Of Woman Born: Motherhood as Experience and Institution.* New York: W.W. Norton & Co., 1976.

Ruddick, Sara. "Maternal Thinking." *Feminist Studies* 6, no. 2, Summer 1980, 342–367.

———. *Maternal Thinking: Toward a Politics of Peace.* Boston: Beacon Press, 1989.

Satir, Virginia. *Peoplemaking.* Palo Alto: Science and Behavior Books, Inc., 1972.

Schumacher, E.F. *Good Work.* San Francisco: Harper & Row, 1979.

Steindl-Rast, David. "Learning to Die." *Parabola* II, no. 1, 1977.

Stendahl, Brita. *Sabbatical Reflections: The Ten Commandments in a New Day.* Philadelphia: Fortress Press, 1980.

Sulivan, Jean. *Morning Light: The Spiritual Journal.* Trans. Joseph Cunneen and Patrick Gormally. Mahwah: Paulist Press, 1988.

Teilhard de Chardin, Pierre. *Hymn of the Universe.* New York: Harper & Row, 1965.

Vanesse, S.J., Alfred. "Religious Language and Relation to the Mother." *Lumen Vitae* **XXXII**, no. 4, 1977, 423–433.

Walker, Alice. "Turning into Love." *Callaloo* 12, no. 4, 663–666.

Willard, Ann. "Cultural Scripts for Mothering." *Mapping the Moral Domain*. Gilligan, Ward and Taylor, eds. Cambridge: Harvard University Press, 1988.